W9-BTZ-456

THE CHRISTIAN AND GNOSTIC
SON OF MAN

STUDIES IN BIBLICAL THEOLOGY

A series of monographs designed to provide clergy and laymen with the best
work in biblical scholarship both in this country and abroad

Advisory Editors:

C. F. D. MOULE, *Lady Margaret's Professor of Divinity
in the University of Cambridge*

PETER ACKROYD, *Samuel Davidson Professor of Old Testament Studies,
University of London*

JAMES BARR, *Professor of Semitic Languages and Literatures,
University of Manchester*

C. F. EVANS, *Professor of New Testament Studies,
King's College, London*

FLOYD V. FILSON, *Formerly Professor of New Testament Literature
and History, McCormick Theological Seminary, Chicago*

G. ERNEST WRIGHT, *Professor of Old Testament History and
Theology at Harvard University*

STUDIES IN BIBLICAL THEOLOGY

Second Series · 14

THE CHRISTIAN AND GNOSTIC SON OF MAN

FREDERICK HOUK BORSCH

ALEC R. ALLENSON INC.
635 EAST OGDEN AVENUE
NAPERVILLE, ILL.

SBN 8401 3064 3
FIRST PUBLISHED 1970
PRINTED IN GREAT BRITAIN

TO BARBARA

CONTENTS

CONTENTS

PREFACE

BECAUSE of the title of my 1967 study and because the designation does occur in several of the gnostic writings and out of a spirit of puckishness, it was tempting to entitle this work 'The Son of the Son of Man'. The present title is, however, no doubt more indicative of the concerns of the book, and I am appreciative of the opportunity to test several aspects of my earlier thesis, especially through materials of the second century AD, in more depth than I was previously able to do.

My thanks are due to Professors Ernest W. Saunders and R. McL. Wilson who read the manuscript, gave me the benefit of their comments and saved me from several errors. Any remaining errors are, of course, the responsibility of the author. I am also grateful to Professor Jack B. Van Hooser and other of my colleagues for their assistance at various stages. Mrs Robert Stahl carefully typed and then retyped the manuscript, and I have been aided in proofreading and compiling indices by Mr Dennis G. Young and Mr John L. Peterson, graduate assistants.

Evanston, Illinois   FREDERICK H. BORSCH
February 1970

ABBREVIATIONS

AThANT	Abhandlungen zur Theologie des Alten und Neuen Testaments, Zürich
ATR	*Anglican Theological Review*, Evanston, Ill.
BG	(Codex) Berolinensis Gnosticus
BR	*Biblical Research*, Chicago
BZNW	Beihefte zur *Zeitschrift für die neutestamentliche Wissenschaft und die Kunde der älteren Kirche*, Berlin
CG	(Codex) Cairensis Gnosticus
FRLANT	Forschungen zur Religion und Literatur des Alten und Neuen Testaments, Göttingen
ICC	International Critical Commentary, Edinburgh
JA	*Journal Asiatique*, Paris
JBL	*Journal of Biblical Literature*, Philadelphia
JTS	*Journal of Theological Studies*, Oxford
NovTest	*Novum Testamentum*, Leiden
NTA	E. Hennecke, *New Testament Apocrypha* (ed. W. Schneemelcher; English editor, R. McL. Wilson) London 1963–5
NTS	*New Testament Studies*, Cambridge
SMMH	F. H. Borsch, *The Son of Man in Myth and History*, London 1967
USQR	*Union Seminary Quarterly Review*, New York
TU	Texte und Untersuchungen zur Geschichte der altchristlichen Literatur, Berlin
TWNT	*Theologisches Wörterbuch zum Neuen Testament* (eds. G. Kittel and G. Friedrich), Stuttgart 1933ff. Now being translated as *Theological Dictionary of the New Testament* by G. W. Bromiley, Grand Rapids, Michigan, and London 1964ff.
ZNW	*Zeitschrift für die neutestamentliche Wissenschaft und die Kunde der älteren Kirche*, Berlin
ZRGG	*Zeitschrift für Religions- und Geistesgeschichte*, Köln
ZTK	*Zeitschrift für Theologie und Kirche*, Tübingen

'There exists Man and the Son of Man.'

(*The Apocryphon of John* and
The Gospel of the Egyptians)

I

THE PRIORITY OF THE SON OF MAN
IN RIVAL PARALLEL SAYINGS

I. THE SEARCH FOR HISTORICAL CONTEXTS

THE impression is sometimes given that redactional and other critical arguments demonstrate conclusively that the great majority of the Son of Man themes in the Gospels are creations by the Christian communities. A number of the scholars who share this impression seem prone to suggest that their viewpoint is confirmed by a consensus created by similar critical arguments. This writer, however, has attempted to show that there is often no such agreement on the basis of fundamental critical considerations. Indeed, while these scholars may, to a degree, share certain beliefs about the background of the Son of Man conception in Judaism along with several hypotheses about the churches' interest in fashioning Son of Man materials, they are frequently in profound disagreement about the *Sitze im Leben* for the formation of the logia and often present contradictory theories regarding the manner and the order in which the sayings came into being.

Of course, these disagreements do not in themselves demonstrate that any one particular theory about the origin of the Son of Man materials is in error. Nor, most certainly, do they invalidate the critical approach to such materials. Neither do they relieve the burden of 'proof' that is upon those who would suggest that certain themes and understandings, though they have, of course, been used and at least reinterpreted when not reformulated by the churches, could derive from pre-Easter contexts (whether 'authentic' to Jesus or not) rather than from the communities formed after Easter. These disagreements do help to remind us, however, that reasonably assured contexts for the earliest forms of these themes may not yet have been found and that there remain many serious anomalies in the several theories about the churches' formulation of the majority of them. Certainly we must also continually remind ourselves that, while it is possible to write a feasible history for the use of every gospel pericope beginning with a *Sitz im Leben* in the churches, this does not mean that such is the most probable context for its origin.[1] (We are thinking here as historians and not as historian-theologians asking questions about the amount of *proven evidence*, if in this arena one ought even to speak in such terms, which, for example, may be required to establish a relationship between the Jesus of history and the Christ of faith.) Disagreements among scholars could indicate that the question of the *most probable* context for the origination of certain of the Son of Man materials remains very much at issue.[2] We here offer but a

---

[1] There is, in other words, a natural bias in most form-critical and redactional/compositional studies to claim as much as seems feasible as grist for their mills. Today while redactional studies are making such great advances, it is perhaps especially important to remember (as, of course, is also true in non-biblical literary studies) that a demonstration of the use of a theme or understanding by an author in his composition is not necessarily a demonstration of its creation by him. Without this continued awareness the study of the Gospels could become a narrowing art distorted by insufficient reference to the wider context of historical movements.

[2] In our earlier study, *The Son of Man in Myth and History* (= *SMMH*), London 1967, we attempted to create a working, historical model by placing two hypotheses close beside one another in order to see if they might enlighten each other in such a way as to give us a better insight into the beginnings of Christianity. We first argued for a more complex context for Jesus' ministry than is usually employed as a basis for discussion. Vital here was the variegated sectarian baptizing movement, portions of which, we believe, were concerned with mythical and 'liturgical' motifs ultimately deriving from stories about the First Man, a figure known both as a lowly, humble creature and as an idealized, royal (sometimes heavenly) hero. Aspects of these beliefs and practices may also have had an influence upon later gnostic understandings. (See also below, pp. 115ff.) In the second place, we tried to indicate how linguistic and environmental criteria indicate that a number of the Gospels' Son of Man logia could reach back to the Aramaic-speaking communities and perhaps even to the very foundations of Christian belief. Many of these sayings, even though they have been fully interpreted with different eschatological and historicizing understandings by the Christian communities, have long provided difficulties just because they bear features exhibiting a remarkable diversity from the *known* concerns and/or language of the *normative* Judaism of the time and of the early churches. Their basic themes are also usually well attested by cross-section or multiple attestation criteria, including an interesting and perhaps highly significant witness from the Fourth Gospel. A number of these essential themes and some of the language used to describe them might then be regarded as more coherent with a background such as that sketched above than with any other life setting. Behind our enquiry there lay two further important questions. (i) In spite of theories to the contrary, would not a Jew in Jesus' time, exercising the sense of authority which

few illustrations of some of these important disagreements, leaving others to be commented upon as we proceed.

Several scholars, while yet claiming at least partial support for their theories from the work of Tödt, are willing to question Tödt's belief[3] that the desire to establish the ἐξουσία of Jesus as the Son of Man was the vital causative factor in the community formation of early sayings regarding the Son of Man on earth.[4] Yet Tödt has made this contention so central and integral to his brilliant and closely argued thesis that he might seem more in danger from his friends than his opponents.

Tödt maintains that Mark 2.10 ('the Son of Man has authority on earth to forgive sins') was taken over from pre-Marcan materials by an evangelist who 'no longer understood the use of the name Son of Man as a designation for Jesus acting on earth with full authority'.[5] But for Norman Perrin this 'is a Marcan emphasis'.[6] Carsten Colpe, countering several decades of insistence that critical arguments militate against the authenticity of the saying, now suggests that it might be from Jesus, though the Son of Man title would then be a misunderstanding of the *bar nash(a)* idiom.[7]

Tödt has also contended that the use of scriptural references in a saying like Mark 14.62 ('You shall see the Son of Man sitting at the right hand of God and coming with the clouds of heaven') represents a relatively late stage in the development of the Son of Man tradition.[8] Perrin, however, insists that the use of these

---

many scholars believe the gospel data reveal, have most naturally sought to associate his ministry with some role bearing some kind of a designation or descriptive reference? (ii) Would not a thesis such as ours help us, working strictly as historians, to come to some better insight into how it was that this astounding idea of Jesus' resurrection was encouraged to take root in the understanding of his earliest disciples?

[3] Cf. H. E. Tödt, *The Son of Man in the Synoptic Tradition*, ET, London 1965, ch. III.

[4] E.g. N. Perrin, 'The Creative Use of the Son of Man Traditions by Mark', *USQR* 23, 1968, 360f., and 'The Son of Man in the Synoptic Tradition', *BR* 13, 1968, 13ff. Here Perrin builds further on his considerable insights into the ways in which the Son of Man themes have been put to use by the evangelists.

[5] Tödt, *op. cit.*, 120 n. 3.

[6] Perrin, *USQR* 23, 1968, 361. See *BR* 13, 1968, 20ff.

[7] C. Colpe, ὁ υἱὸς τοῦ ἀνθρώπου, *TWNT* VIII, 433, and see further below.

[8] Tödt, *op. cit.*, 37, 66.

quotations should be seen as the key to the beginning of the whole phenomenon.[9]

Similarly, Tödt argues for the relative lateness of Mark 13.26f. ('And then they will see the Son of Man coming in clouds with great power and glory'),[10] while Perrin apparently regards the logion as evolving from some of the earliest Christian productions.[11] Bultmann and others infer that it may well have been taken over from a pre-Christian Jewish way of speaking.[12]

Howard Teeple is among those who advocate a position much like that maintained earlier by Bultmann, that many of the other Son of Man sayings were formed in the Hellenistic churches.[13] But Tödt, and now many another, point to the indications that a number of these same logia seem to have originated in an environment where Aramaic was the spoken language.

Philipp Vielhauer has contended that sayings like Matt. 11.19 (= Luke 7.34: 'The Son of Man came eating and drinking . . .') and 8.20 (= Luke 9.58: 'Foxes have holes and the birds of the air have nests; but the Son of Man has nowhere to lay his head') are inauthentic.[14] Tödt agrees and sees this question of Jesus' ἐξουσία as the Son of Man as vital to their formation.[15] A. J. B. Higgins suggests that Matt. 11.19 is authentic as an 'I' saying, but that Son of Man as a title has been intruded into it.[16] Fuller is prepared to admit this as a possibility for both Matt. 11.19 and 8.20, while agreeing with Higgins, Tödt, etc., that the passages are not to be explained as resulting from the misunderstood *bar nash(a)* idiom.[17] Perrin, however, argues emphatically for the authenticity of Matt. 11.19 suggesting an original use of the *bar nash* idiom as an indirect

[9] N. Perrin, *Rediscovering the Teaching of Jesus*, London 1967, 173ff., and BR 13, 1968, 3–5. For another view of Mark 14.62, cf. F. H. Borsch, 'Mark 14.62 and I Enoch 62.5', NTS 14, 1967/8, 565ff.

[10] Tödt, *op. cit.*, 66.

[11] Perrin, *Rediscovering*, 184.

[12] Cf. R. Bultmann, *The History of the Synoptic Tradition*, ET, Oxford 1963, 122. In another context, Tödt (*op. cit.*, 35f.) would seem to find this view compatible with his thesis.

[13] H. J. Teeple, 'The Origin of the Son of Man Christology', JBL 84, 1965, 213ff.

[14] Vielhauer, 'Gottesreich und Menschensohn in der Verkündigung Jesu', in *Festschrift für Günther Dehn* (ed. W. Schneemelcher), Neukirchen 1957, 51ff. Cf. also his 'Jesus und der Menschensohn', ZTK 60, 1963, especially 163ff.

[15] Tödt, *op. cit.*, 115f., 123f.

[16] Higgins, *Jesus and the Son of Man*, London 1964, 123ff.

[17] R. H. Fuller, *The Foundations of New Testament Christology*, New York 1965, 43, 124f.

reference to Jesus' own person.[18] Joachim Jeremias has now contended that the idiom would not have meant 'I' in Matt. 11.19 and that Matt. 8.20 cannot be regarded as an instance of the misunderstood idiom.[19]

2. JEREMIAS' CATEGORIES

It is to the recent arguments of Jeremias that we now wish to turn, confining most of our observations to them. Jeremias has rightly drawn our attention again to the significant number of Son of Man logia that have parallels in which the title is missing. He finds grounds for holding that the latter have priority over the former and ends his article by suggesting that the Son of Man sayings without rival parallels may well be of great significance for our understanding of the origins of the Son of Man traditions. Obviously the contention that Matt. 8.20 par.; 10.23; 24.27 par.; 24.37(39b) par.; 25.31; Mark 13.26 parr.; 14.62 parr.; Luke 17.22, 30; 18.8; 21.36 and John 1.51 may be significant for an understanding of the formation of other Son of Man sayings would play havoc with the theses of several of the scholars mentioned above.[20] Here, however, it remains our essential purpose to question Jeremias' own theory.

Jeremias puts forward four categories by means of which the development of the Son of Man logia with rival parallels can be

[18] Perrin, *op. cit.*, 120f.

[19] Jeremias, 'Die älteste Schicht der Menschensohn-Logien', *ZNW* 58, 1967, 159ff. In essential respects we agree with Jeremias' view (*op. cit.*, 165 n. 9) that the *bar nash(a)* idiom was probably not a genuine first-person circumlocution, though it evidently could be employed to refer to the speaker in contexts in which he was thinking of himself as one of the 'any man' to which the idiom could also refer. (See Borsch, *SMMH*, 23 n. 4, with reference to the important article of G. Vermes, 'The Use of the Bar Nash/Bar Nasha in Jewish Aramaic' in M. Black, *An Aramaic Approach to the Gospels and Acts*[3], Oxford 1967, 310ff.) In this view, context will be the all important consideration, and we agree with Jeremias that 'a man/any man' would be unlikely to make good sense in a saying lying behind Matt. 8.20. Indeed, although it is possible to find different nuances in such a saying, we hold that the same would be still more true for Matt. 11.19. Colpe, however (*op. cit.*, 408, 433ff., 455ff.), stands somewhat nearer to Vermes when he holds that the idiom may be involved in five or six gospel logia including Matt. 8.20 and 11.19, both of which he believes may be authentic.

[20] Jeremias' insights and whole approach have found considerable support from Colpe, who argues for the likelihood of a background of authenticity in the sayings Matt. 10.23; 24.27 par.; 24.30a; 24.37 par.; Luke 17.30; 18.8; 21.36; 22.69 parr. In our view, however, the greatest merit of Colpe's article is found in his redactional interpretations indicating the ways in which the evangelists have made use of the earlier Son of Man themes.

understood: (1) A few are the result of a misunderstanding of the *bar nasha* idiom where originally it was intended to mean 'anyone' or 'a man'. (2) Others are modifications of older logia so as to include the Son of Man designation. (3) Some are secondary copies of older Son of Man sayings. (4) A few others are entirely new formations making use of the title. Actually, however, most of the parallels that we find to be of genuine significance for this discussion are explained by Jeremias under categories (1) or (2). Either we can agree with him about the majority of the materials to be placed in categories (3)[21] and (4)[22] or (and this is the case with many of the examples he brings forward) the proposed parallels are too vague or too partial to be of genuine help in this discussion. In these latter instances little evidence is available indicating that we are dealing with true parallels, and the employment of one or two common words in different sayings could be used to *prove* any number of things in particular cases. It might suggest that the words or themes involved reach back to earliest tradition and/or that later formulations have borrowed from the Son of Man materials.[23] We are particularly impressed through our studies by the manner in which several of the Son of Man themes and their specific vocabulary tended otherwise not to be widely used by the churches.[24] In any event, the language sometimes reveals

[21] See *SMMH*, 317ff., for example, on Matt. 26.2 and Luke 24.7 and the significant reasons suggested for these later formulations.

[22] The existence of a slight tendency in sub-apostolic times to create new sayings employing a title so significant in the Gospels is hardly surprising. What surprises most is the slightness of the tendency! We shall find it far more interesting that the designation had coinage in certain gnostic circles which also evidence other signs of derivation from the earlier sectarian milieu. A pericope like Gospel of Philip, saying 54 (see below, pp. 78f. and 111 n. 197), could be regarded as under the influence of either or both of these conditions. We cannot, however, accept Jeremias's suggestion that a textual variant as at Matt. 25.13 indicates an ongoing tendency. That some scribe should add 'in which the Son of Man comes' to a saying which already 'sounded' like other Son of Man logia (e.g. Luke 12.40 par.) does not seem a truly significant factor in this discussion. Other poorly attested textual variants referring to the Son of Man are found at John 5.19, 25; 6.56. (Son of Man was apparently altered to Son of God in John 9.35.) On Luke 9.56a and Matt. 18.11 with Luke 19.10, cf. *SMMH*, 326ff. The textual evidence indicates no real development in this direction.

[23] It seems methodologically unstable, for example, to suggest that 'the Son of Man must be lifted up' language (John 3.14; 8.28; 12.34) might be regarded as secondary to John 12.32. Cf. Jeremias, *op. cit.*, 163; Colpe, *op. cit.*, 473 n. 462.

[24] See *SMMH*, ch. VI–VIII, and below in ch. II and III.

distinct signs of having first been predicated of the Son of Man.[25]

Other than the logia to be discussed below, the only saying which, on our view, has pertinence to the central concern of this discussion is Mark 2.10 (= Matt. 9.6; Luke 5.24). Jeremias revives the suggestion (though he admits to genuine qualms) that Matt. 9.8 ('. . . the crowds . . . glorified God, who had given such authority to men') can tell us something about the original meaning of a saying which lies behind Mark 2.10: '. . . The Son of Man has authority on earth to forgive sins'. Though *bar nash(a)* could not have meant simply 'I' (see above), it may have been the phrase originally employed here and may presumably, as Matthew might seem to indicate, have been intended to indicate that *a man* has authority on earth to forgive sins.

Colpe also takes up this possibility in a tentative fashion, though he recognizes that Matt. 9.8 would then represent a secondary, interpretive and somewhat mistaken tradition,[26] for, according to Colpe,[27] Jesus was here essentially contrasting himself as *a man* with God. This would mean that the saying with the 'son of man' expression was primary, and the central concern would focus on the manner in which this expression was first intended. Here, however, we agree with those critics who, though often questioning the authenticity of the saying, believe that a definite claim to the authority of a special role must have been fundamental to the formation of the logion,[28] and we would still hold that John 5.27 ('[God] has given him authority to make judgment because he is the Son of Man')[29] may be the true 'parallel' to a

[25] Jeremias' suggestion, for instance, that many of the Son of Man passion sayings could be later parallels to logia which do not have the designation might be questioned by his own recognition of the strongly primitive character of Mark 9.31a. On the recognition that Mark 9.31a reaches back to an Aramaic and very early level of tradition, cf. further W. Popkes, *Christus Traditus: eine Untersuchung zum Begriff der Dahingabe im Neuen Testament* (AThANT 49), 1967, 258ff. While Colpe, too, stresses the primitive character of certain of the themes now associated with the Son of Man in passion statements (*op. cit.*, 446ff.), he also believes that the Son of Man title was later inserted into some of these materials. We cannot see, however, that he has found any genuine criteria for so arguing.

[26] Colpe, *op. cit.*, 463.

[27] Colpe, *op. cit.*, 433 n. 236.

[28] Cf. *SMMH*, 321 n. 2.

[29] Also on the earthly *man* 'having authority' (cf. Gen. 1.26, 29; Ps. 8.6) while yet himself subject, cf. *Corpus Hermeticum* I.15 quoted below, p. 70 n. 50. The authority to make judgment is also, of course, characteristic of the Son of Man in I Enoch, cf. I Enoch 69.27.

saying like Mark 2.10. In addition, we do not find that the suggested use of the idiom in this context would meet the criterion
for its employment outlined above (i.e. that the idiom would by
inference suggest that other men beside the speaker would share
in his circumstances and capacities), for, if it were to be so interpreted, the statement would then seem strikingly un-Jewish.

On this same basis it would seem unlikely that the Aramaic-
speaking Jewish Christian churches would have held that 'men'
have the authority to forgive sins, as Matt. 9.8 contends. The verse
appears more readily explicable as a Matthean (or late tradition)
expansion in line with sayings like Matt. 16.19 and 18.18. Indeed,
redactional and form-critical arguments would seem to indicate
that Matt. 9.8 has all the marks of an editorial supplement,
especially as a final comment confirming the miraculous character
of the event through the crowd's awe.

3. ELEVEN PARALLEL SAYINGS

We come, then, to the eleven important sayings which, in our
opinion, form the essentials of Jeremias' thesis. We shall here
focus our attention on the issue of primacy, for the most part
leaving questions about 'authenticity' with Jesus aside. In order to
try to establish grounds for objectivity we shall seek to employ,
where applicable, some of the traditional critical standards for
attempting to adjudge primacy: (*a*) shorter; (*b*) 'harder'; (*c*) more
'source' witnesses; (*d*) from a more reliable 'source'; (*e*) more
reflective of Aramaic vocabulary and/or grammatical patterns.[30]

1.	Luke 12.10	Matt. 12.31f.	Mark 3.28f.
	And every man who speaks a word against the Son of Man will be forgiven; but he who blasphemes against the Holy Spirit will not be forgiven.	Therefore I tell you, every sin and blasphemy will be forgiven men, but the blasphemy against the Spirit will not be for-given. And whoever says a word against the Son of Man will be forgiven; but whoever speaks against the Holy Spirit will not be forgiven, either in this age or the age to come.	Truly, I say to you, all sins will be forgiven the sons of men and whatever blasphemies they utter, but who-ever blasphemes against the Holy Spirit never has forgiveness, but is guilty of an eternal sin.

---

[30] The use of several of these characteristics has now been criticized by
E. P. Sanders, *The Tendencies of the Synoptic Tradition* (Society for NT Studies,
Monograph Series 9), Cambridge 1969. His criticisms are often pertinent,

These verses, as is well known, present us with an exceedingly complex situation.[31] This is the only one of the eleven 'rival' sayings, which we shall now study, that Jeremias would explain as the result of a misunderstood idiom. This argument is usually made either on the basis that the Marcan version is more faithful to the original saying, or it is contended that the Marcan version can at least give us some insight into the intention of the original logion.[32]

We, however, find, in the first place, that the Marcan version is probably secondary to that of 'Q'. Though inconclusive of itself, many scholars, given a choice like this, would favour the Q version on the grounds of the general primitiveness of the Q material.[33] Also the Q version, since it is employed by both Matthew and Luke, must have existed in such a form prior to the evangelists' use of it, while there is no such guarantee in the case of the Marcan version. More than this, a number of scholars who normally favour the two-document hypothesis at least recognize how difficult it is to reconcile these passages with that theory. Often they seek to remedy the difficulties by suggesting the possibility of two versions of Q or the existence of another source for either the Matthean or Lucan version of the saying using the Son of Man.[34] If this theorizing is tenable, there were, then, two lines of tradition behind the saying with the Son of Man and perhaps only one for the logion without the designation.

The Q version of the saying fits well with the context given by Mark himself (accusations against Jesus), while the present Marcan version is quite anomalous in this regard. This certainly raises the suspicion that it is Mark or his tradition which has tampered with the earlier thrust of the logion. In addition, the Q version offers a strong and obvious parallelism which disappears in the Marcan saying.[35]

---

and one can rarely speak of 'laws' in this area. Unfortunately his study arrived too late to affect the body of this work.

[31] For representative views and for further discussion of points mentioned below, see *SMMH*, 328f.

[32] Cf. Colpe, *op. cit.*, 445.

[33] Tödt, *Son of Man*, 312, points out that Wellhausen's theory was based on his belief that Mark represented a generally more reliable tradition than Q.

[34] Cf. F. W. Beare, *The Earliest Records of Jesus*, Oxford 1962, 102. See also the next note on the Gospel of Thomas version which seems obviously to be based on a saying using a title.

[35] There is another version in the Gospel of Thomas, log. 44. There, in what is obviously a late and much-revised tradition, blasphemy against the

On this basis we hold the basic form of the Q version to be primary. But what of the possibility that the Marcan version can tell us something of the intention of the logion now best preserved by Q? This theory could be based on the feasibility of an original Aramaic logion in which *bar nasha* was susceptible to different interpretations while both Mark and Q may present legitimate attempts to translate the grammar of the Aramaic.[36] Thus, although on the grounds given above Q may present a superior rendering of the structure of the logion, this saying may originally have intended, 'Every one who speaks a word (blasphemes) against a man will be forgiven . . .' Now, this we regard as being a very interesting possibility, since it appears to us as the only logion in the Gospels which would meet the criterion set out in our preceding discussion for the use of the idiom as a kind of first-person circumlocution: i.e. Jesus is here speaking primarily of himself in the light of the accusations made, though the same remark could legitimately be applied to all men. Either this, or, as some scholars hold, the idiom was only intended to apply to mankind generally.

One might, however, ask (though the point is far from conclusive) whether Jesus would ever have made such a remark with these implications. It is not just that it does not seem very fitting

---

Father and the Son will be forgiven. It is significant, however, that this version decidedly reflects the form and parallelism of the Q saying and not the structure of the Marcan logion. Though R. McL. Wilson (*Studies in the Gospel of Thomas*, London 1960, 148) feels that there may have been a progression from the Marcan through the Q version to that of Thomas, any suggestion that the Thomas traditions can tell us about early Christian understandings must here reckon with this basic relationship to the Q form.

[36] R. Schippers in 'The Son of Man in Mt. 12.32 = Lk. 12.10 compared with Mk. 3.28', *Studia Evangelica* IV (TU 102, ed. F. L. Cross), 1968, 231ff., suggests: *kol (ma'n) dīgaddēp barnāšā yišt*bēq lēh.* The 'Marcan' tradition understood this as 'All that which men blaspheme will be forgiven unto them' and rendered it 'All will be forgiven unto men which soever they blaspheme'. The Q tradition read, 'Whosoever shall blaspheme the Son of Man it will be forgiven unto him' and rendered it 'Whosoever shall speak a word against the Son of Man, it will be forgiven unto him'. Though Schippers sees both sides of the argument, he recognizes that 'there are solid reasons to suggest that Q gave the right interpretation', which it was right to understand in at least a quasi-titular sense. It is interesting (see Colpe, *op. cit.*, 445 n. 302) that a use of *lamedh* before *bar nasha* in a slightly different version of the Aramaic ('All blasphemies . . .' or 'All which is said . . .') might still leave the ambiguity, since it might be understood either as 'on the part of' (or perhaps 'for') or as 'against'.

that one with a message such as his should, to this degree, make it possible for men to speak against one another, but, more importantly, it would appear grossly to contradict (if authentic) Matt. 5.22f. where those who say ῥακά to their brothers are liable to the council and those who say μωρέ are worthy of Gehenna.

There also remain grounds for questioning the possibility that Mark's version is 'legitimately' derived from the Aramaic. The Q version is considerably 'harder', and one could well wonder if the absence of parallelism in Mark is not a sign of an attempt to manage the difficulties felt to be present in the Q version. While a theory like that of Tödt's *may* account for the creation of such a Q saying by the church, even he then holds that the Marcan version is a later attempt to deal with it.[37] In this light one can point again to the awareness that Mark's version does not well accord with its context, perhaps indicating a late editorial alteration. Tödt also entertains the suggestion, in the light of Mark 2.27, that Mark (or his reviser) may have been prone to generalize on the basis of Son of Man statements.[38] In addition, though 'to blaspheme' can be seen as a translation variant along with 'to say a word against',[39] it is the latter which seems more faithful to the Aramaic and Tödt presents strong reasons for seeing 'to blaspheme' not only as a later and quasi-technical term of the churches but also as a possible proclivity of the evangelist himself.[40]

None the less, although in the debate regarding rival parallel sayings the Q version with the 'son of man' expression stands out in several ways as primary, the possibility remains that it was not first intended in any sense which would call to mind the titular designation now found frequently throughout the Gospels. Those who contend that the saying is authentic, while disputing the idea that Jesus in any way associated himself with the role of the Son of

[37] Tödt, *op. cit.*, 120. We do not believe, however, that the original saying envisioned two periods of the salvation drama. We have argued that this is a tortured and untenable interpretation, though see Colpe, *op. cit.*, 456. Compare also Schippers, *op. cit.*, 234: 'We can imagine a situation in which it was impossible for G[=the tradition behind Mark and Matt. 12.31] to translate *bar nasha* in this logion by the Son of Man.'

[38] Tödt, *op. cit.*, 131 n. 2. Matt. 9.8 might be another such by the church.

[39] So Schippers, *op. cit.*, 233. M. Black, *Aramaic Approach*, 194f., regards 'to say a word to' (εἰς: Luke) or 'against' (κατά: Matt.) as 'a Semitism, and probably Aramaic in origin'. This might shed some light (see above) on a hypothetical use of *lamedh*.

[40] Tödt, *op. cit.*, 315f.: 'It is evident from this survey that "to blaspheme" does not occur in the earlier strata of the synoptic tradition.'

Man, will probably hold that this must have been the case. Others, however, perhaps agreeing that this would be the only instance of the misunderstood idiom (possibly wondering whether Jesus would have made such a statement which could be understood to refer to all men) and recognizing that Q is otherwise to be credited with preserving the original force of the saying (and perhaps also believing that Jesus could have associated his mission with the Son of Man figure, and/or seeing certain affinities with a saying like Luke 6.22)[41] may well wish to hold that the present Q version is superior in every way.

2.	Luke 11.29f.	Mark 8.12	Matt. 16.4
	This generation is an evil generation; it seeks a sign, but no sign shall be given to it except the sign of Jonah. For as Jonah became a sign to the men of Nineveh, so will the Son of Man be to this generation. (Similar is Matt. 12.39f. with additions.)	Why does this generation seek a sign? No sign shall be given to this generation.	An evil and adulterous generation seeks for a sign, but no sign shall be given to it except the sign of Jonah.[42]

There are no certain grounds for maintaining the priority of either the Marcan or Q version. While one could point to the general respect for the primitiveness of Q material and the willingness by Bultmann, Tödt, Higgins and others even to regard the saying as authentic and coherent with Jesus' message, it is also true that significant scholarship has long questioned this view.[43]

[41] For, of course, it is possible in both passages that the statement originally referred to the heavenly Son of Man, whose followers are persecuted on account of their Son of Man beliefs, as perhaps also in I Enoch.

[42] The inclusion of 'except the sign of Jonah' by Matthew in his second version of this pericope, and in a context where he may otherwise appear to be following Mark, cannot be used to argue that he knew yet another version of the logion, since he may only be employing the sign to refer to his earlier interpretation of the saying, i.e. except for the death and resurrection.

[43] E.g. J. M. Creed, *The Gospel according to St Luke*, London 1930, 162f. Though some have suggested that the Marcan syntax seems to demand some kind of a conclusion, others would see it as reflecting a strong form of Semitic denial or oath of denial (though even then some form of an apodosis is usual). On the other hand, while some would argue that the absolute refusal of a sign could reflect an authentic attitude on the part of Jesus, others would find this absolute denial to be a Marcan redactional emphasis with

It might, however, seem that Mark or his tradition has become shorter through the dropping of the difficult allusion and analogy. Certainly others hold that Mark must have omitted at least the reference to Jonah, and we will content ourselves with quoting from Tödt's argument: the 'enigmatic addition "except the sign of Jonah" was hardly inserted subsequently.[44] There must therefore have occurred in Q a saying in which Jesus rejected the demand for a sign, and said that only the sign of Jonah would be given. This must have been followed, then, by a saying stating some kind of analogy . . .'[45]

3.	Matt. 24.43f. (= Luke 12.39f.)	Gospel of Thomas logion 21b	Gospel of Thomas logion 103
	. . . if the householder	If the Lord of the house	Blessed is the man
	had known in which part of the night the thief was coming, he would have watched	knows that the thief is coming, he will stay awake	who knows in which part the robbers will come in, so that he will rise and collect his ( ) and gird up his loins
		before he comes	before they come in.
	and would not have let his house be dug through into.[46]	and would not let them dig through into his house of his kingdom to carry away his goods.	
	Therefore you must also be ready;	You then must watch	

reference to 'this generation' of Jews. It is, in other words, the 'Q' version which may in context appear 'harder'.

[44] So W. G. Kümmel, *Promise and Fulfilment*, ET², London 1961, 68. See Colpe, *op. cit.*, 452; Perrin, *Rediscovering*, 193: 'The sign of Jonah saying itself is certainly authentic.' Perrin is also in disagreement with Vielhauer (*ZTK* 60, 1963, 150f.), holding the following material about Nineveh and the queen of the South (Luke 11.31f. = Matt. 12.41f.) to be 'certainly dominical' (*op. cit.*, 195). Such could be true even if 'Q' has used these sayings with reference to its understandings regarding a contemporary mission to Gentiles.

[45] Tödt, *op. cit.*, 211. It does not seem satisfactory, with Colpe and others, to view Jesus' reference to Jonah as though it were intended to be a kind of mystery. The analogy, as explained by Tödt, is reasonably clear, forceful and can be seen to harmonize well with sayings that Jeremias and Colpe regard as primitive.

[46] This thoroughly Palestinian conception (cf. T. W. Manson, *The Sayings of Jesus*, London 1949, 116f.), evidently based on an Aramaic expression (J. Jeremias, *The Parables of Jesus*, ET², London 1963, 48 n. 1), is preserved also by Luke and the Coptic. The Coptic could reflect the original Aramaic, but it may also be based on the Greek of the Gospels or another source or possibly reflect a Syriac version.

	for the world, gird up your loins	gird up his loins (see above)
for the Son of Man	with great strength lest the robbers find a way	
is coming	to come to you,	before they come in (see above).
	because they will	
at an hour	find the advantage	
you do not expect.	which you expect.	

A continuing process of the construction of Son of Man sayings, for which Jeremias argues with respect to other known channels of transmission, was evidently avoided by the Gospel of Thomas.[47] This writer must also confess to his understanding that the material in this Gospel has gone through considerably more recensions than some other scholars would recognize, as even a comparison with the Oxyrhynchus papyri seems to indicate. There is a proclivity to give a shorter version of other sayings found especially in Matthew and Luke and then to fill them out with somewhat gnostic observations. There is also a tendency to eliminate or soften eschatological remarks and to lay stress upon the present, inward character of salvation in the kingdom.

None the less, setting such prejudgments aside, the question could remain as to whether Q or one of the Gospel of Thomas versions best preserves the earliest form of the saying. It might be tempting to think that the shortest form (Thomas, logion 103) should be the most original, but, while Thomas, logion 21b, seems to reveal some acquaintance with the ending offered by logion 103,[48] it even more evidently witnesses to knowledge of a longer version bearing quite a few features in common with the

[47] Log. 86 presents its only Son of Man saying and this is a parallel to Matt. 8.20 = Luke 9.58. Rather would we suggest that Thomas does fit into the picture by making more evident a process which we see happening in other sources – a tendency to drop the Son of Man designation. See above, p. 9 n. 35, and below, pp. 83f.

[48] Jeremias (*Parables*, 49, 95) suggests that this ending is the result of an interweaving with motifs from Luke 12.35ff. which might indicate the relative lateness of these endings. A version of Matt. 12.29 seems also to have entered into the composition of log. 21b. B. Gärtner in *The Theology of the Gospel according to Thomas*, New York 1961, 42, points out that the tendency to conflate material from the Gospels is found frequently among other gnostics as well as elsewhere in the early church. Gnostics especially liked to give new meanings to old texts in this fashion. In this regard cf. Hippolytus, *Refut.* V. 8.11, on which see below, p. 72.

Q passage. (And, of course, the Q witness would be doubled if there was more than one version of 'Q'.) On these grounds it would seem safest to believe that there was an earlier version of more length than logion 103 now indicates. Thus, on our view, the issue really comes down to a contest between the Q version and that of Thomas logion 21b. Now, however, it is Q which is favoured as being the shorter and which is even regarded as authentic and coherent with other authentic materials by critics like Tödt and Fuller.[49] If they are correct, the reference to the Son of Man may well have been omitted[50] by Thomas for the purpose of permitting an 'improved' gnostic interpretation[51] and/or by the more literal-minded in order to avoid the seeming comparison of the Son of Man with a thief.[52] The version in

[49] Tödt, *op. cit.*, 54; Fuller, *Foundations*, 123. See Kümmel, *Promise and Fulfilment*, 55f.

[50] Note that Rev. 3.3b also appears to know a version of this tradition in which the thief is compared to the eschatological figure. In this case, however, it is 'I' = Jesus rather than the Son of Man. Cf. below, pp. 32f.

[51] It is typical of the gnostic approach to parabolic materials to omit interpretive elements found in the Gospels in order to enable a new, 'secret' understanding to stand forth. Here, as elsewhere in gnostic literature, the lord of the house is the gnostic believer, the house is the inner reality of the kingdom and the thief (or thieves) is the corrupting world. For more on this gnostic character and the explanation of the details without reference to a special, independent source, cf. Gärtner, *op. cit.*, 171–82; R. M. Grant with D. N. Freedman, *The Secret Sayings of Jesus*, Garden City, N.Y., 1960, 142 and especially W. Schrage, *Das Verhältnis des Thomas-Evangeliums zur synoptischen Tradition und zu den koptischen Evangelienübersetzungen* (BZNW 29), 1964, 67–69.

[52] At I Thess. 5.2 the comparison, perhaps significantly, is with 'the day of the Lord' and not the Lord himself. On I Thess. 5.2 and this passage, cf. further *SMMH*, 361 n. 1. Colpe, though rightly challenging the suggestion that a comparison with Matt. 24.42 ('you do not know on what day your Lord is coming') shows v. 44 to be original, does recognize that v. 44 should be accounted primary. Indeed, these comparisons suggest it is quite early. Jeremias contends (*Parables*, 49) that 'the application of the parable to the return of the Son of Man is strange: for if the subject of the discourse is a nocturnal burglary, it refers to a disastrous and alarming event, whereas the *Parousia*, at least for the disciples of Jesus, is the day of great joy'. Yet this might well argue for the primitive character of the analogy, since a number of the Son of Man sayings, regarded by Jeremias himself as early, sound this motif of warning and possible disaster. (Nor can we accept Colpe's objection, *op. cit.*, 454 n. 360, that the accent here lies on the process of keeping watch with a view toward an imminent event and not on the person of the coming one, since he accepts as very early a number of sayings which emphasize both themes.) While the logion may be interpreted so as to deal with the delay in the *parousia* (and doubtless the churches would have done so), this, in the light of comparable sayings, need not have been its original intent. Jeremias (*op. cit.*, 50), finding the symbol of the thief to be 'foreign to the

logion 21b was then completed with themes and a non-eschatological point of view otherwise fully consistent with the Gospel of Thomas.

4.	Luke 12.8		Matt. 10.32
	Everyone who acknowledges me before men, the Son of Man will also acknowledge before the angels of God.		Everyone who acknowledges me before men, I also will acknowledge before my Father who is in heaven.

Jeremias offers only the inference that, if in other sayings with rival parallels the Son of Man is secondary, so it must be here as well. Here, however, he is contradicted by the great majority of scholars who deal with the sayings, whether they regard Luke 12.8 as authentic or not. The only other sure point of contrast in the sayings is provided by 'before my Father who is in heaven' versus 'before the angels of God'. All seem to agree that the latter phrase has the best chance of being primitive[53] and that the other is clearly Matthean. One may also point to the association between the Son of Man and angels elsewhere.[54]

The most interesting alternative possibility is set forth by Perrin[55] when he suggests an original saying (perhaps authentic)[56] which, however, used a passive verb without any reference to the Son of Man: 'Everyone who acknowledges me before men will also be acknowledged before the angels of God.' Curiously, however, Perrin would buttress this possibility with reference to the passive form in Luke 12.9, a logion which he nevertheless holds to be secondary to 12.8 and which, he believes (quite rightly, we shall argue below), was itself once known in a version which employed the Son of Man designation as the subject of an active verb. Indeed, since both Mark 8.38 and Matt. 10.33 seem to know a version of Luke 12.9 which was expressed actively, and since

---

eschatological imagery of late Jewish literature', infers that Matt. 24.43 is an authentic motif. Surely, then, one need hardly have been fully *allegorical* in making an analogy with the startling appearance of the Son of Man.

[53] E.g. Perrin, *op. cit.*, 188f.

[54] In the Gospels (note especially John 1.51), I Enoch and in connection with the activities of a number of other Adamite figures. Cf. also Dan. 7.10.

[55] Perrin, *op. cit.*, 185ff. Cf. Vielhauer, 'Gottesreich', in *Fest.-Dehn*, 68f.

[56] We do not fully understand, however, how and why Perrin (*op. cit.*, 190f.) believes that Jesus would have felt justified in making such a claim unless he saw himself in relation to some divinely appointed role or office, i.e. more than a prophet or a herald of the kingdom.

Luke 12.8 and Matt. 10.32 are only known in active forms,[57] reason would seem to be on the side of suggesting that the earliest form of Luke 12.9 was active as well. A subject is therefore required and, since Luke 12.8 already has the Son of Man as a subject, and since Mark 8.38 seems an independent witness to such a subject, it appears most likely that the Son of Man was the original subject in Luke 12.9.[58] It now is doubly significant that Matthew has 'I' in lieu of the Son of Man in his 10.33 as well as in 10.32.

Perhaps Perrin's argument might be amended as follows: (1) The original Luke 12.8 was in the passive without the Son of Man. (2) Luke 12.9 was now formed on this model. (3) The double saying was then transformed into two Son of Man sayings by the 'Lucan' tradition (thus helping to give rise to Mark 8.38) and into two 'I' sayings in the Matthean tradition. (4) Because, however, of a continuing awareness of the earlier version of Luke 12.8f., one strand of tradition caused Luke 12.9 to revert to a passive form.

While we agree that the use of the passive with God understood as the agent is often the sign of a primitive saying, this does not, of course, mean that it must have been employed wherever it might have been. Thus, although suggestions such as Perrin's cannot be ruled out, all else (including the possibility of an original play on men or sons of men/Son of Man)[59] indicates a fully Semitic[60] pair of distichs exhibiting both internal and external

[57] Also active is Rev. 3.5b, which seems to have knowledge of this tradition. Since, however, this version refers to 'before my Father' and 'before my angels', it appears to have been aware of both the 'Matthean' and 'Lucan' versions. A study of Rev. 3.5b in context may, however, help us to see how and why the churches' usage transformed Son of Man materials into 'I' sayings. Here the former would be awkward and ambiguous, but the latter provides a very satisfying pronouncement. Cf. below, pp. 33f.

[58] I. H. Marshall, 'The Synoptic Son of Man Sayings in Recent Discussion', *NTS* 12, 1965/6, 344, suggests that Luke may have altered 12.9 in his redactional process in order to build a better bridge to v. 10.

[59] The chance that the variance between 'I' and the Son of Man resulted from a misunderstanding of *bar nasha* would, of course, here be denied by Jeremias and others. It is also militated against by the agreement of Matthew and Luke in certain key Greek phrases, suggesting that the alternative arose in a Greek-speaking church.

[60] With regard to the criticisms of ἀρνέομαι see below on our preference for the 'ashamed' in Mark 8.38. Perrin, *op. cit.*, 187f., points to the Aramaic background of ὁμολογήσῃ ἐν ἐμοί and ὁμολογήσει ἐν αὐτῷ.

Though it does not directly affect the question of priority, Perrin's

parallelism. Such a double-saying this critic and others, from our differing points of view, find consonant with the background materials and well supported by sayings with a similar import.[61]

> He that acknowledges me before men/
> The Son of Man will acknowledge him before the angels of God.
> He that is ashamed of me before men/
> The Son of Man will be ashamed of him before the angels of God.

5. Mark 8.38 (similar is Luke 9.26)	Luke 12.9	Matt. 10.33
For whoever is ashamed of me and of my words in this adulterous and sinful generation, of him will the Son of Man also be ashamed when he comes in the glory of his Father with the holy angels. (Cf. Matt. 16.27)	but he who denies me before men will be denied before the angels of God.	but whoever denies me before men, I also will deny before my Father who is in heaven.

We have already indicated our reasons for believing that Luke 12.9 once included an explicit reference to the Son of Man, a saying on which Matt. 10.33 is a variant. It is difficult to see why Mark 8.38 would include a reference to the Son of Man unless this were so.[62] Mark has then filled out the primitive logion with 'and

---

suggestion (*op. cit.*, 22f., 186, following Käsemann) that such sayings could well be inauthentic because they follow a pattern used elsewhere by the early churches e.g. (I Cor. 3.17; 14.38) would be more effective if it could be shown that this form was used only by the Christian communities. In fact, however, the form of a two-part pronouncement, employing the same verb in each part, with the first part stating an activity of man and the second stating or inferring a divine eschatological activity is certainly to be found in Mark 11.25f. (cf. the inverse order in the Lord's Prayer, Matt. 6.12f. par.), in Matt. 5.7 (and perhaps was at one time used in other of the beatitudes as well) and several times in Luke 6.37f.

[61] See below on these themes in I Enoch. Cf. Borsch, 'Mk. 14.62 and I Enoch 62.5', *NTS* 14, 1967/8, 565ff. One of the more interesting defences of the authenticity of Luke 12.8f. is provided by Wolfhart Pannenberg, *Jesus – God and Man*, ET, Philadelphia 1968, 59f.

[62] So Tödt, *op. cit.*, 339: 'We have to note that the sole variant of Luke 12.9, the Marcan version of the saying, does contain the name Son of Man, obviously without being dependent on a version in Q.' See also Kümmel, *Promise and Fulfilment*, 45 n. 86.

If II Tim. 2.12b is another variant of this saying (which we consider unlikely), it probably shows an even greater adaptation of the logion along the lines of Matt. 10.33. See below, pp. 34f.

of my words in this adulterous and sinful generation'. It could be concluded that the rest of the saying is also Marcan expansion using the 'before the angels of God' as a starting-point and including a mention of the idea of the Son of Man's coming. We have, however, given what we believe are strong reasons for believing that Mark has, in fact, conflated a version of a Son of Man saying now paralleled in Luke 12.9 with another Son of Man tradition now reflected by Matt. 16.27 ('For the Son of Man is to come with his angels in the glory of his Father . . .') which Matthew (because he was following his own source of tradition here) did not so conflate. We have argued that such an understanding of Mark's redactional work would give us an excellent insight into the manner by which Mark 8.38 came into existence.[63]

We have also suggested above that the Marcan 'ashamed' better preserves the original intention than does the 'deny' in Luke 12.9 and Matt. 10.33 which is at least suspect as a translation or reinterpretation conditioned by church usage.[64] While the motifs of retribution for those who deny or are ashamed of the Son of Man[65] and reward for those who affirm him are generously represented in I Enoch, it is the theme of being confounded or ashamed which comes particularly to the fore.[66] One may single out I Enoch 63.11.[67]

[63] See *SMMH*, 380. Note especially, whatever theory is held with regard to the composition of these sayings, that Mark 8.38 and Matt. 16.27 speak of 'his Father' (i.e. the Son of Man's Father) while Matt. 10.32f. uses 'my Father'. The former surely appears more primitive and even awkward from the Christian point of view, as Luke 9.26 seems to indicate.

[64] Cf. Vielhauer, 'Gottesreich', in *Fest.-Dehn*, 70, and *ZTK* 60, 1963, 142; Perrin, *op. cit.*, 187. The verbs could, however, be regarded as translation variants pointing back to an Aramaic logion; they might also reflect an early error, HPR vs. ḤPR.

[65] The being ashamed of one representative of the Son of Man on earth might well be compared with the themes of the Son of Man's rejection and treatment with contempt as in Mark 8.31 and 9.12 and frequently in stories about Adamite figures. (Compare also Matt. 8.20 = Luke 9.58.) With reference to the King figure see Pss. 69.7, 17; 89.45. Compare especially Isa. 50.6 and the carrying forward of this theme in Mark 10.34.

[66] Cf. I Enoch 46.4–8; 48.4–10; 62.5–16; 63.7–11; 69.26–29. The theme is well established in the OT, with God as subject bringing men to shame especially in connection with judgment. The language here is also reminiscent of the Enochian-like introduction to Matt. 25.31ff. Compare especially Matt. 25.41.

[67] J. C. Hindley has rightly drawn our attention again to the problems which are raised when one tries to give a definitive pre-Christian date to the Similitudes of Enoch; see 'Towards a Date for the Similitudes of Enoch. An

And after that their faces shall be filled with darkness
And shame[68] before that Son of Man,
And they shall be driven from his presence . . .

6.   Mark 8.31 (= Luke 9.22)   Matt. 16.20f.

And he began to teach them that the Son of Man must suffer many things, and be rejected . . .

. . . he strictly charged the disciples to tell no one that he was the Christ. From that time Jesus began to show his disciples that he must go to Jerusalem and suffer many things . . .

Few, if any, would question the likelihood that it is Matthew or his tradition which has here dropped the reference to the Son of Man. Jeremias and others, however, have attempted to undermine the significance of this by pointing to the Matthean 'insertion' of the title at 16.13. Yet, as we have argued before,[69] if Matthew intended the Son of Man designation to be understood at 16.21, his intention is not at all clear. An *independent* reading of Matthew at this point shows that he has moved the Christ title to the fore, however much he has also come simply to identify Jesus with the Son of Man.

7.   Matt. 16.13   Mark 8.24 (= Luke 9.18)

When Jesus came into the district of Caesarea Philippi, he asked his disciples, 'Who do men say that the Son of Man is?'

'Who do men say that I am?'

Again, despite the theory that Matthew has here inserted the title in order to stress Jesus' role as the sovereign Son of Man,[70]

Historical Approach', *NTS* 14, 1967/8, 551ff. His own arguments for a date early in the second century AD, however, even when taken as a whole, do not seem very compelling. It would appear that the bulk of the material in the Similitudes simply cannot be readily dated in relation to known historical events. In any case, there remains little or no evidence that this section of I Enoch was influenced by Christianity, and we continue to regard it as a form of parallel testimony to the development of a concern with the Son of Man.

[68] *Ḥafret.* See the very similar statement made about the Lord of Spirits' judgment in I Enoch 62.10. This word (compare Hebrew and Aramaic ḤPR) is also used in the Ethiopic NT at Mark 8.38.

[69] *SMMH,* 378f.

[70] Cf. Tödt, *op. cit.,* 150.

we believe that the Matthean narrative indicates that the evangelist and probably the tradition before him were deflecting the original import of the material in the direction of their concern with Jesus' Messiahship. Matthew's account, read independently, leaves the Son of Man designation very much up in the air. This ambiguity seems also to have been experienced by scribes who altered Matt. 16.13, apparently under the influence of the Marcan and Lucan versions.

Furthermore, as we have argued in some detail, the linkage between the Son of Man, Elijah, John the Baptist and Jesus, which is present in this passage, has a vital place in the very early traditions of the churches.[71] However much the communities have attempted to reinterpret these associations, they probably ought not to be dismissed as wholly new creations within the traditions. A concern with 'who the Son of Man is' (i.e. who on earth might represent the Son of Man in this age?) may have played an important role in earlier circumstances.

8.	Mark 9.1 (= Luke 9.27)	Matt. 16.28
	Truly, I say to you, there are some standing here who will not taste death before they see the kingdom of God come with power.	Truly, I say to you, there are some standing here who will not taste death before they see the Son of Man coming in his kingdom.

As is the case with the preceding logion, some would dismiss the possible priority of the Matthean saying on the basis of the theory that, where Matthew and Mark share parallel material, Matthew always has Mark for his only source. One might believe, however, that there are at least a sufficient number of dubieties about the two-document hypothesis for such a rigid approach to need always to be questioned. Only in this way can the tools of form and redactional criticism be allowed the freedom of exercise that they deserve.[72] In any event, in the particular section Matt. 16.13ff. we have found a number of reasons for believing that Matthew may have been using another source (which perhaps

[71] Cf. *SMMH*, 372ff. See there also (381f.) on the manner in which a reconstruction of the entire passage from the Caesarea Philippi scene through the verses following the transfiguration might reveal a thorough-going interest in the Son of Man as well as a recurrence of the concern for the link between the Son of Man, Elijah, John the Baptist and Jesus.

[72] On this point cf. W. R. Farmer, 'The Two-Document Hypothesis as a Methodological Criterion in Synoptic Research', *ATR* 48, 1966, 380ff.

already included the special Petrine material). One significant factor is the possibility that Matt. 16.27 is more original to this context than is Mark 8.38. As indicated above, Mark 8.38 seems more readily explicable as a conflation of a saying like Luke 12.9 and Matt. 16.27a than is Matt. 16.27a explicable as having been extracted by Matthew from Mark.

So, too, there are strong reasons for believing that it is Matt. 16.28 which better preserves an earlier saying than does Mark 9.1. The Matthean version retains a continuity of thought which Mark 9.1 breaks so severely that the latter has regularly been regarded as an interpolation. Far more importantly, the language of both Matt. 16.28 and Mark 9.1 is better suited to a Son of Man logion than to a statement about the kingdom of God. However much Matthew *may* have adapted the saying to his own point of view, we are accustomed from I Enoch,[73] Daniel and the Gospels[74] to hear of *seeing* the Son of Man *coming*. Such language is, at best, associated with the kingdom of God in a very limited and probably secondary manner.[75]

9.	Luke 6.22	Matt. 5.11
	Blessed are you when men hate you, and when they exclude you and revile you, and cast out your name as evil, on account of the Son of Man.	Blessed are you when men revile you and persecute you and utter all kinds of evil against you falsely on my account.[76]

---

[73] On *seeing* the Son of Man, who goes with the Head of Days and appears on his throne, cf. I Enoch 46.2, 4; 62.5; 69.29.

[74] On his *coming* (ἔρχομαι) see Mark 8.38 par.; 13.26 parr.; 14.62 par.; Luke 7.34 par.; 12.40 par.; 18.8; 19.10; Matt. 10.23; 16.27; 25.31; cf. Rev. 1.7. On seeing him, cf. Mark 13.26 parr.; 14.62 par.; John 6.62 and note Luke 17.22; 17.24 par.; 17.30; John 1.51; Acts 7.56; Rev. 1.7; 14.14. The thought is frequently implicit where not explicit.

[75] Outside of the much more Jewish idea of the kingdom drawing near or becoming established, there is the use of φθάνω with the kingdom in Matt. 12.28 par. Ἔρχομαι is employed at Matt. 6.10 par. and here in Mark 9.1 (and we should perhaps consider Mark 11.10). The idea appears to gain in Luke 17.20f.; 22.18. Luke 17.20f. is an interesting case because, apart from the question of its authenticity, it seems to suggest that the kingdom will not be *seen coming*. (On seeing the kingdom or its appearance cf. significantly and only Luke 19.11; John 3.3 and here at Mark 9.1 par.) Indeed, such an idea might even be regarded as nearly anomalous as far as the kingdom is concerned.

[76] We cannot see how a consideration of Mark 8.35 would be of much help in this discussion. If anything, Mark 8.35b would indicate the kind of materials the churches were creating which would have helped to influence an earlier version of Luke 6.22 in the direction of a logion like Matt. 5.11.

The priority of the Lucan version is maintained by Vielhauer, Beare, Manson, Higgins and others.[77] While Luke may have somewhat recast the form of the saying[78] and additions to the types of persecutions could easily have been made by him or others (note especially the reference to being *excluded*), he is regularly regarded as having better preserved the Aramaic flavour of the logion.[79] While, of course, such does not guarantee that he has not substituted the Son of Man, there appear to be no form-critical or redactional critical reasons for suggesting that he has done so.[80] Indeed, the Lucan version may seem to exhibit again the characteristic ambiguity evidenced in other sayings regarding Jesus' relationship to the Son of Man figure. Similarly, there is here the theme of future reward, and the logion can be seen to echo sentiments found in both Daniel and I Enoch.[81] In addition, one may again detect a possible play on men/Son of Man.

10.	Mark 10.45 (= Matt. 20.28)	Luke 22.27d
	For the Son of Man also came not to be served but to serve, and to give his life as a ransom for many.	. . . but I am among you as one who serves.[82]

[77] Vielhauer, 'Gottesreich', in *Fest.-Dehn*, 52; Beare, *Earliest Records*, 96; T. W. Manson, *Sayings*, 56ff.; Higgins, *op. cit.*, 119.

[78] Bultmann, *History of the Synoptic Tradition*, ET², New York 1968, 110, and others have held that the second person form of the beatitude is secondary; but this is far from certain. Cf. *SMMH*, 328 n. 2; Manson, *op. cit.*, 47; Black, *Aramaic Approach*, 157: 'As Luke preserves the more primitive form of Q and in both Matthew and Luke the words are addressed to the disciples, the second person may have been original throughout.'

[79] Black (*op. cit.*, 135, 191) and others point especially to ἐκβάλωσιν τὸ ὄνομα ὑμῶν ὡς πονηρόν. Manson holds that Matthew can be seen to be making his version more edifying while Luke has retained the starker, more eschatological tenor.

[80] Colpe's contention (*op. cit.*, 446 n. 308) that ἕνεκεν ἐμοῦ belongs to an earlier class of additions than ἕνεκα τοῦ υἱοῦ τοῦ ἀνθρώπου asks for a degree of precision that is not ours (especially since 'on account of the Son of Man' is nowhere else instanced), if, as his argument demands (i.e. Luke never inserts the title on his own initiative), the additions were made independently in the traditions prior to the evangelists. Surely, however, it is better to reason that 'on account of . . .' was already involved in the common tradition and that one 'source' or another has altered its object. Indeed, then, on Colpe's own argument, a tendency for ἕνεκεν ἐμοῦ had some strength in the churches, not least in Matthew, and may have prevailed here.

[81] See Dan. 7.13f. with 7.21f., 25–27; I Enoch 46; 48; etc.

[82] Of course, not all grant that these are truly parallel sayings, but the argument of Lohse, mentioned below, convinces us that these are independently derived from the same piece of tradition, while it is yet possible that Mark 10.45 and Luke 22.27 were independent additions to the earlier sayings.

There are, of course, any number of views held with regard to these passages and the ways in which the sayings could have been formed. Many scholars are agreed that Mark 10.45b must have been formulated in an Aramaic-speaking situation;[83] some then go on to suggest that v. 45a should also be seen as coming from such a context. Tödt is among those[84] who see in the pattern of correspondence behind Mark 10.42–45a and Luke 22.24–27 indications that both stem along independent lines from a common tradition to which, he suggests, Mark 10.45b was added. Previous to this, however, the Son of Man was made the subject of 10.45a, while the 'I' of Luke is more primitive. Such a viewpoint can be bolstered by a consideration of the possibility that Luke has better preserved the earlier context for the pericope, i.e. in association with the Last Supper traditions. (If, however, this is so, one may at least wonder if Luke has not *lost* a version of something like Mark 10.45b, since this seems even more firmly linked with such understandings.)[85]

This type of argument would, of course, be undermined if one should follow those who maintain that Mark 10.45a was formed in a Hellenistic-speaking environment.[86] Then it might seem neces-

---

[83] More recently see Popkes, *Christus Traditus*, 170f., and also on the relationship with I Tim. 2.6. Also cf. E. Lohse, *Märtyrer und Gottesknecht* (FRLANT, nF 46), 1955, 118f. If I Tim. 2.5f. is based on Mark 10.45, it might appear once again that later tradition has dropped or transformed (Lohse, *op. cit.*, 119) the title. See also below, p. 36. The primitive character of Mark 10.45b is maintained even by those who see no association with Isa. 53.10, 12. Cf. C. K. Barrett, 'The Background of Mark 10.45', in *New Testament Essays* (ed. A. J. B. Higgins), Manchester 1959, 1ff.

[84] Cf. Tödt, *op. cit.*, 208ff.; Lohse, *op. cit.*, 118.

[85] So M. Hooker, *The Son of Man in Mark*, London 1967, 145 n. 2, points out that it is the Marcan version which might better fit the Lucan context than Luke's version. Thus Mark 10.45b is often viewed in relationship with Mark 14.24. H. Conzelmann, *The Theology of St Luke*, ET, London 1960, 201, suggests that Luke had his theological reasons for omitting Mark 10.45. It is also held that Luke could have reconstructed v. 27 in his attempt to fit the material into the Last Supper tradition, while the anomaly of Jesus serving at the table instead of presiding (compare John 13.1ff.) is sometimes mentioned. Cf. Higgins, *op. cit.*, 37f.

[86] Cf. Higgins, *op. cit.*, 42; Popkes, *op. cit.*, 171. (Bultmann, *op. cit.*, 144, of course, regarded the whole of Mark 10.45 as a Hellenistic formulation.) This consideration is largely based on the absence of διακονέω in the LXX. One might, however, suggest that διακονέω was used in an attempt to soften the harshness (cf. H. W. Beyer, *TWNT* II, 83) that the use of δουλεύω would have conveyed, even though the nuances of the latter might seem more in keeping with the parallelism (see below) in the verses. (Notice, too, that Luke appears to have ὁ διακονῶν in 22.26b in contrast to Mark's δοῦλος.) While δουλεύω often

sary to hold that Mark 10.45b was the earlier statement and that the Son of Man may or may not have been its original subject. This, in turn, might or might not suggest that Luke or his tradition once knew of such a statement about the Son of Man's mission.

In these circumstances, it might seem best for our immediate purposes to confine the comparison to the statements in Mark and Luke which actually appear to be parallel, i.e. Mark 10.42–45a versus Luke 22.25f., 27d. Here, although he still holds that the 'I' of Luke 22.27d is more original, Tödt recognizes that the Christian use of the Son of Man designation might fit well enough with the theme of correspondence established in the preceding verses,[87] and he rightly makes the comparison with Matt. 8.20 = Luke 9.58. (For our purposes here this comparison is useful on any view of Matt. 8.20 which would regard it as extant as a logion predicated of the Son of Man before or at the time of the formation of Mark 10.45a as a Son of Man saying.) Fuller maintains that 'in other respects, however, the Lucan form is less primitive, for it reflects a later concern for church order'.[88] In other words, it appears to us that, while the question of the priority of the Son of Man or of 'I' in the early version of some saying about one who serves is not readily decided on the basis of traditional critical criteria and must be concluded on the broader basis of one's understandings of the

---

translates *ᶜebed* in the LXX, the apparent inability of the Aramaic *ᶜebed* to convey the above idea in a passive sense (cf. J. A. Emerton, 'Some New Testament Notes', *JTS* ns 11, 1960, 334f. – though the power of religious-poetic expression to give words a new emphasis must not be overlooked) would suggest, if this is indeed a translation, that another Aramaic word was involved. On the Aramaic background and also with Mark 9.35 par. in view, cf. Black, *Aramaic Approach*, 218ff.; 228f.

[87] Also on the earthly man as lowly, subject and as a δοῦλος in the creation, see again *Corpus Hermeticum* I.15, quoted below, p. 70 n. 50. On the wider background for this theme, cf. *SMMH*, ch. III–V.

[88] Fuller, *Foundations*, 176 n. 29; see his *The Mission and Achievement of Jesus*, London 1954, 57, and also Lohse, *op. cit.*, 119; F. Büchsel, *TWNT IV*, 341 (Luke is 'obviously' later in style and form) and J. Jeremias (with W. Zimmerli), *The Servant of God*, ET², London 1965, 104 n. 474. (It may have been the concern with church order which caused the ransom reference to be dropped as irrelevant.) And certainly it is Mark rather than Luke who may be seen to preserve the Semitic form of parallelism in Mark 10.44 which may extend to at least part of v. 45. We can, for instance, see a tristich with a vigorous synthetic parallelism, the first two stichs of which are synonymous: 'Whoever would be great among you must be your servant/whoever would be first among you must be slave of all/for even the Son of Man is come not to be served but to serve.'

use of the Son of Man designation in the whole tradition,[89] the factors which do point to the secondary character of Luke's passage cannot make it easy to assert that Luke should be preferred in the subject-matter of this statement.[90]

11. Matt. 19.28	Luke 22.28–30
Truly, I say to you, in the new world, when the Son of Man shall sit on his glorious throne, you who have followed me will also sit on twelve thrones judging the twelve tribes of Israel.	You are those who have continued with me in my trials; as my Father appointed a kingdom for me, so do I appoint for you that you may eat and drink at my table in my kingdom, and sit on thrones judging the twelve tribes of Israel.[91]

A number of scholars suggest that, while these two passages ultimately derive from a common piece of tradition, they were not taken by Matthew and Luke from a common source. Although there are some critics who view Luke as having better preserved the subject of the earliest form of the saying,[92] many others are convinced that Matthew's version is more primitive on this and other accounts,[93] some of them also contending that such a saying is basically authentic.[94] Although Matthew's use of the semi-technical παλιγγενεσία seems a later interpretation, this could be

[89] This applies also to Jeremias' feeling that 'The Son of Man is come . . .' (see Matt. 11.19 = Luke 7.34; Luke 9.56; 19.10; cf. Gospel of Philip, saying 54) is invariably a sign of secondary or newly formulated material, especially as he himself gives good grounds for recognizing the 'is come' type language as a part of the early tradition. See Jeremias, 'Die älteste Schicht', 166. Cf. also *SMMH*, 245, 366 n. 1, 372ff.

[90] It is of some interest that, in his arrangement, Luke follows 22.27 with another pericope which in a rival parallel – from another source – has the Son of Man designation. Has Luke or his tradition omitted the title in both cases?

[91] If Rev. 3.21 is another parallel, Bultmann (*op. cit.*, 159 n. 4) would seem correct in regarding it as a late, universalizing version of the tradition. Thus it would be another indication of a tendency to drop the title. Cf. below, pp. 35f.

[92] E.g. E. Schweizer, 'Der Menschensohn', *ZNW* 50, 1959, 189. The reference to eating and drinking could be viewed as a primitive motif preserved by Luke, but on eating with the Son of Man in paradise, see I Enoch 62.14. See also below, p. 35 n. 14.

[93] Cf. Bultmann, *op. cit.*, 159; Vielhauer, 'Gottesreich', in *Fest.-Dehn*, 61; Kümmel, *Promise and Fulfilment* ('undoubtedly'), 47; Tödt, *op. cit.*, 62ff.

[94] Kümmel, *ibid.*; Fuller (*Foundations*, 123) chides Tödt for abandoning his method in his rejection of the saying. From his very different point of view, Vielhauer also regards Tödt as inconsistent in regarding Matt. 19.28 as inauthentic, since it is congruous with other relatively primitive sayings in its *seeming* distinction between Jesus and the Son of Man.

seen as more than balanced by the presence of the Semitic 'throne of his glory' which is also firmly linked with the Son of Man in I Enoch.[95]

The briefer form of the Matthean version may also tell in its favour and the Lucan references to continuing 'with me in my trials'[96] and the conception of Jesus ruling in 'my kingdom' appointed by his Father contrast sharply with the Matthean reference to the Son of Man sitting on '*his* throne'. Whether or not Matthew's version was created by those who exclusively identified the Son of Man with Jesus, the Lucan version bears many indications of having been rephrased to do away with any ambiguities. It is not easy to see this aspect of the process moving in the other direction.

4. CONCLUDING REMARKS

As a result of these analyses we find that the various tools of source, form and redactional criticism tend to point, sometimes rather conclusively, to the priority of the Son of Man designation in traditions where there are probable parallels without the Son of Man. (The exceptions must be Matt. 16.13 and 16.28, where, however, unless the theory that Matthew has only Mark for a source in cases where he parallels Mark is rigidly adhered to, there

---

Normally Jeremias would regard the Matthean introductory ἀμὴν λέγω ὑμῖν as a sign of authenticity. (See Jeremias, 'Characteristics of the *ipsissima vox Jesu*', now in *The Prayers of Jesus*, London 1967, 112ff., 115 n. 47.) Here, however, it may only be borrowed from Mark 10.29. On the other hand, one may wonder if 'Mark' has not omitted this saying because of its exclusiveness, while retaining the introduction.

[95] I Enoch 47.3; 62.2, 5; 69.27; cf. 45.3; 51.3; 55.4; 61.8. Note also 108.12b, where the loyal followers are all seated upon thrones. Since the phrase 'throne of his glory' and the Son of Man are also found in Matt. 25.31, some regard such as indications of Matthean editorial activity. Yet the idea of thrones is common to both versions of this pericope. This and the other indications of the primitiveness of the Matthean version, together with the stereotyped character of the reference to the Son of Man sitting on the throne of his glory, suggest the pre-Matthean character of these motifs as part of this tradition.

[96] On this as an obvious Lucan theme, cf. Conzelmann, 'Zur Lukasanalyse', *ZTK* 49, 1952, 29 n. 1, who seems in *Theology of St Luke*, 117, to accept the secondary character of Luke here. On the 'sign of inferior tradition' in Luke's omission of the mention of *twelve* thrones, see Higgins, *op. cit.*, 108 n. 3, and Tödt, *op. cit.*, 64. Luke or his tradition might well have wished to *unlimit* the number of thrones and thus provide a more general promise for later Christians. See also Tödt, *op. cit.*, 63 n. 1, on the primitive character of the twelve theme.

are signs indicating that even here the Son of Man was the prior subject.) Although one readily admits that the evidence regarding a saying like Luke 12.10 par. versus Mark 3.28f. par. is susceptible to different interpretations, we do not find a single case where it can be said that the balance of evidence would dictate the opposite conclusion. While the outlook of Jeremias and Colpe is fresh and interesting, if the Son of Man is to be seen as secondary in these traditions, it must be done, in our opinion, with relatively little help from fundamental critical tools and on the basis of other arguments.

But, it may be asked, is there a theory which, in contrast to those of Jeremias, can account for this rather striking phenomenon of some eleven pericopes which speak of the Son of Man all having parallels which do not? Is there a theory which would also account for the other instances, listed by Jeremias, in which language elsewhere associated with the Son of Man now is otherwise employed or predicated of Jesus by name, pronoun or by another designation? We hold that there is; and it is the same theory to which, as we shall see, much other evidence outside the Gospels points as well. While we agree that the evangelists have often been careful to preserve this title so honoured in their sources,[97] the Son of Man conception can be understood as a genuinely formative influence only in the primitive strata of tradition or earlier, after which it ceased to be, outside of preserved traditions, part of the normative language of the churches. Intervening, however, there were stages in which there were tendencies, examples of which we have noted above, to drop, supplement, interpret[98] or replace the designation either for reverential reasons or with direct and unambiguous references to Jesus[99] or with more familiar titles like Lord or well-known themes such as the kingdom of God.

[97] See Jeremias, 'Die älteste Schicht', 168. This, however, is not always pertinent to the present discussion, since, as we have seen, in most if not all cases under consideration the differing versions may have been or most likely were extant in the traditions which the evangelists received.

[98] On the possibility of a tendency to interpret or translate 'the Son of Man' with references to 'the man', 'man' or 'men', see on Matt. 9.8; Mark 2.27; 3.28f. (cf. above, p. 11) and I Tim. 2.5f. (cf. above, p. 24 n. 83). On I Cor. 15.21, 47; Rom. 5.15, etc., and perhaps Phil. 2.7, see *SMMH*, 240ff.

[99] This latter tendency might seem especially evident in Rev. 3.3b (with Matt. 24.43f. par.); 3.5b (with Luke 12.8 par.) and 3.21b (with Matt. 19.28 par.). Also, of course, compare Rev. 1.7 with Matt. 24.30. On all these passages see in the subsequent chapter.

II

THE SON OF MAN IN EARLY
CHURCH LITERATURE

WHATEVER the theory employed to account for the widespread, varied and deeply rooted position of the Son of Man designation in the canonical Gospels, the relative infrequency of the title in other early, *non-gnostic* Christian literature has often been the occasion for comment if not for statements of genuine surprise. It is the purpose of this chapter to examine passages outside of the Gospels where the title does occur and to seek better to understand the reasons for reference to the figure in these pericopes. We shall also study some significant contexts in which the designation does not appear. Then we shall attempt to draw conclusions from our research.

First, we shall look at several passages in the canonical New Testament. The area of interest will then be extended to more or less orthodox Christian literature of the immediate sub-apostolic period. (Our cut-off date will be approximately the middle of the second century.) We shall also examine later literature which may contain material formulated in apostolic or sub-apostolic times. Materials which might fairly be classified as being as much or more *gnostic* than *orthodox* Christian will at this stage be excluded from our range of interest.[1]

[1] The attempt to classify early Christian literature as either *orthodox* or *gnostic* is, of course, fraught with difficulties and in some instances more than a little academic. It is beyond question that many Christians of this period would have been unable so to separate themselves in any clear-cut fashion. *Gnostic* proclivities and beliefs have affected writings which we shall here examine, and more than a few of the *gnostic* authors retained a perspective which was at least as much Christian as it was dominated by attitudes and understandings which inform writings of a more decided gnostic character. Nevertheless, important differences in terms of cosmology, anthropology and ethics do exist which enable us, however tentatively or arbitrarily in some cases, to frame certain categories, and it serves our purposes to divide the

I. IN THE ACTS, EPISTLES AND REVELATION

This author has commented elsewhere on Acts 7.56; Heb. 2.6; Rev. 1.13 and 14.14, and it will suit our purposes here but to summarize those findings.[2] While it remains possible that Stephen's exclamation in Acts 7 is a vestige from some movement or movements which created certain of the Son of Man logia in the Gospels, it appears more likely that the reference to the Son of Man is a function of Luke's creativity as he modelled this scene on features associated with the passion of Jesus. Stephen, like Jesus, also speaks of the eschatological hero before the 'Sanhedrin'.

Heb. 2.6 contains a mention of υἱὸς ἀνθρώπου in a quotation of Ps. 8.4–6 amid a catena of Old Testament references. The anarthrous usage does not seem significant in itself and shows no contact with any of the passages in the Gospels.

Rev. 1.13 and 14.14 also contain anarthrous mentions of the figure (as in Daniel: '*like* a Son of Man') and also reveal no direct points of reference with either synoptic or Johannine materials. They are probably better explained as dependent upon Jewish apocalyptic materials.[3]

While there are a number of Pauline passages where one might have expected to read the designation,[4] it is not found in his epistles. Whether or not Paul was even acquainted with the Son of Man tradition could be debated. Also a subject of debate is the question as to whether Paul may have at points dropped the designation or translated it as 'the Man'. It would appear, however,

---

relevant material roughly in this manner. It will be our next task, however, to examine much of the gnostic corpus and to see if and why a different impression is there to be gained regarding the use of the Son of Man designation.

[2] See *SMMH*, 232ff.

[3] The possibility that the seer is borrowing from older Jewish tradition might appear enhanced by the lack of clarity with regard to the figure's identity in 14.14f. (R. H. Charles, *The Revelation of St John* [ICC], 1920, vol. II, 20–23, held vv. 15–17 to be a later interpolation.) In connection with synoptic material it is, however, interesting to compare Mark 13.27 (= Matt. 24.31) and especially Matt. 13.41 in the light of Matthew's preceding parable. Although one might contend that there is here some direct connection between Matthew and Revelation, the several differences in the presentation, the widespread usage of harvest imagery in Judaism (as also elsewhere in the Gospels) and the dependence of the seer throughout this passage on common Jewish apocalyptic imagery suggest that both Matthew and the Seer were separately dependent on this general fund of ideas. Compare Joel 3.13.

[4] On this and the matters mentioned below, cf. *SMMH*, 240ff.

that Paul took no part in the creation or preservation of Son of Man sayings.

In the Book of Revelation there are several significant sayings lacking any direct reference to the Son of Man which yet strongly resemble Gospel logia where the title is to be found. Rev. 1.7 is beyond question linked with a tradition that involves Mark 13.26 (= Luke 21.27; cf. Mark 14.62 parr.) and its longer parallel Matt. 24.30. The Marcan text is ultimately based on language found in Dan. 7.13f., while Revelation and Matthew have also made use of Zech. 12.10ff. Reference to the Zechariah passage is also made in John 19.37.

And then they will see the Son of Man coming in clouds with great power and glory. (Mark 13.26)

And again another scripture says, 'They shall look on him whom they have pierced.' (John 19.37)

Then will appear the sign of the Son of Man in heaven, and then all the tribes of the earth will mourn, and they will see the Son of Man coming on the clouds of heaven with power and great glory. (Matt. 24.30)

Behold, he is coming with the clouds, and every eye will see him, every one who pierced him; and all the tribes of the earth will wail on account of him. (Rev. 1.7)

Most commentators regard Matt. 24.30 as a direct development of the tradition evidenced by Mark 13.26 and see Rev. 1.7 as a yet later version or at least another secondary formulation in comparison with both. Though this is not certain,[5] whatever view is held in this regard, it must still be abundantly clear that the tradition on which Rev. 1.7 is ultimately based once contained a direct reference to the figure coming with the clouds as the Son of Man.

[5] Some of the variations in presentation (*with* [μετά] or *on* [ἐπί] or *upon* [ἐπάνω]; see below in Justin and *Did.* 16.8] the clouds of heaven or *in* [ἐν] clouds; compare Dan. 7.13: ʿim-ʿanānē šᵉmayyā = ἐπί or μετά the clouds of heaven) may indicate points of contact with different interpretations of Aramaic tradition. Helmut Köster, *Synoptische Überlieferung bei den apostolischen Vätern* (TU 65), 1957, 184–90, especially 188 n. 3, suggests that Rev. 1.7 is not derived directly from Matt. 24.30, but rather uses language from Jewish apocalyptic which was also employed by Matthew in expanding the original Marcan version of Mark 13.26. In any event, we notice that Rev. 1.7 does agree with Mark 14.62 in speaking of μετά the clouds rather than ἐπί the clouds as in Matt. 24.30.

It is not, however, easy to understand why the reference has
been dropped. There seems insufficient relationship with 1.13
merely to contend that the designation has been postponed until its
more descriptive usage in the second context. In the light of the
three verses next to be discussed one may guess that the tradition
behind the Revelation was handed down by Christians not particularly interested in this designation as a title no longer employed
in worship and preaching. It had, therefore, already been omitted
from this particular pericope.

There are three remnants of tradition in the third chapter of the
Revelation which arouse interest. The first is Rev. 3.3b.

But know this, that if the householder had known in what part of
the night the thief was coming, he
would have watched and would not   If you will not watch, I will come
have let his house be broken into.   like a thief, and you will not know
Therefore you also must be ready;   at what hour I will come upon you.
for the Son of Man is coming at an   (Rev. 3.3b)
hour you do not expect. (Matt.
24.43f.)

There continues to be some debate as to whether the 'Q' passage
(see Luke 12.39f.) is a reasonable facsimile of the earliest form of
this logion. Comparisons with I Thess. 5.2, 4 and II Peter 3.10
and now also with the Gospel of Thomas, logia 21 and 103, have
caused scholars to ask if the understanding of the thief as the Son
of Man is not a later addition.[6] We have earlier argued that this is
not the case,[7] but even that issue is really secondary here, for Rev.
3.3b stands much closer in form and language to Matt. 24.43f. than
any of the other passages in question, and seems to share in that
particular form of the tradition. In I Thessalonians and II Peter the
comparison is with the 'day of the Lord',[8] while the Gospel of
Thomas pericopes also avoid comparing the eschatological hero
with a thief. Rev. 3.3b appears to presuppose a tradition in which
the eschatological figure (at some point having been identified
with Jesus) was so analogized. Moreover, only the Q and Revelation passage link this comparison with a specific reference to the

---

[6] See Jeremias, *Parables*, 49f.; 'Die älteste Schicht', 168; Colpe, *TWNT*
VIII, 454ff.
[7] Cf. above, pp. 13ff.
[8] Compare Matt. 24.42; Mark 13.33, 35.

unexpected 'hour'.[9] It is, of course, conceivable that the tradition of Revelation is more primitive than that of Matthew, but the relative superiority of the Q material would suggest the greater likelihood that the Son of Man has been identified with Jesus and become 'I' rather than that the inverse process has taken place.

This general movement in the tradition might also seem to be corroborated by Rev. 3.5b.

So everyone who acknowledges me before men, I also will acknowledge ($\delta\mu o\lambda o\gamma\eta\sigma\omega$ . . . $\dot{\epsilon}\nu$) him before my Father who is in heaven. (Matt. 10.32)	and I will acknowledge ($\delta\mu o\lambda o\gamma\eta\sigma\omega$) his name[10] before my Father and before his angels. (Rev. 3.5b)	Everyone who acknowledges me before men, the Son of Man also will acknowledge ($\delta\mu o\lambda o\gamma\eta\sigma\epsilon\iota$ $\dot{\epsilon}\nu$) him before the angels of God. (Luke 12.8)

Again, we have elsewhere contended (with many others) that the presence of the Son of Man in Mark 8.38, parallel with Luke 12.9; Matt. 10.33, together with other considerations, indicates that the reference to the Son of Man is more indigenous to this tradition than the direct 'I' reference.[11] This, however, offers no guarantee that the Seer or his tradition has deliberately dropped the Son of Man designation, since obviously he could have been using the form of tradition now found in Matthew. On the other hand, it also seems clear that the reference to both 'my father' and the 'angels' shows some association with both renderings of the tradition. This could be accounted for by suggesting that the Revelation form is more primitive and that the Matthean and Lucan versions have borrowed different elements from that

[9] Rev. 16.15 is probably to be regarded as another instance of the same tradition, the specific reference to the 'hour' having been dropped in this brief interjection. It is also interesting, however, that both the Thomas logia and Rev. 16.15 have a reference to being clothed in preparation. *Did.* 16.1 also joins together the themes of *girding up* and the coming of the Lord. This may be coincidence, since the being clothed image is presented in different language in Rev. 16.15 (Thomas and *Didache* probably being dependent on Luke 12.35) and is frequent generally in early Christian literature, but it might also be a sign of some other (probably late) form of tradition.

[10] The variation 'his name' instead of 'him' is accounted for by v. 5a: 'He who conquers shall be clad thus in white garments, and I will not blot *his name* out of the book of life.'

[11] This could be true even if the original form of the saying contained passive verbs implying divine activity. On this matter and the gospel parallels generally, see above, pp. 16ff.

tradition.[12] Yet the secondary character of Rev. 3.5b appears confirmed by its lack of reflection of the Aramaic idiom in the expression ὁμολογεῖν ἐν.

It would seem, then, that there is at least a strong possibility that the author of Revelation or the source of his material knew of a tradition which spoke of 'the Son of Man acknowledging'. This he either altered or treated as less useful in comparison with another tradition, the subject of which was 'I'. In either event the usage would have been strongly influenced by the general form of 'I' soliloquy in these chapters of Revelation. As perhaps Matthew (or his tradition) also felt in the context of his Gospel, 'the Son of Man' here would have sounded distinctly ambiguous and out of keeping while the direct 'I' was satisfying and congruous. At the least, Rev. 3.5b again reveals no tendency to add the Son of Man designation to traditional materials.

We should also at this point glance at II Tim. 2.12b: 'If we deny him, he also will deny us'. This eschatological judgment saying, incorporated into a short Christian hymn, could conceivably echo a tradition found in slightly different forms in the synoptics.

| ... whoever denies me before men, I also will deny before my Father who is in heaven. (Matt. 10.33) | ... he who denies me before men will be denied before the angels of God (Luke 12.9) | For whoever is ashamed of me ... of him will the Son of Man also be ashamed when he comes in the glory of his Father with the holy angels. (Mark 8.38 = Luke 9.26) |

Once again we are confronted by a complex situation where, however, we have already argued that the primitive logion had the Son of Man for the subject of an active verb for which 'be ashamed' and 'deny' could be translation variants. II Tim. 2.12b would point to the active form with an eschatological figure as subject, but it is evident, in this case, that the author could be following a Matthean-like rendering of tradition which already

[12] One does notice that Mark 8.38 also couples references to the Father and angels (though we have accounted for this by maintaining that Mark 8.38 is, in fact, a conflation of versions of Luke 12.9 and Matt. 16.27). Such might be used to argue for yet another line of tradition, in which case, however, we must remember that Mark 8.38 is also predicated of the Son of Man in a witness which seems independent of Luke 12.8f.

spoke of Jesus as the subject in terms of a pronoun. Thus, while the author of II Timothy (or the author of the hymn which he has used) could have known a version with the Son of Man as subject, in this instance it is far from certain that the passage by itself is witness to a tendency to drop the title. Certainly, however, it once more indicates no proclivity at this stage in the life of the churches to make new use of the Son of Man designation.

We may now return to the third chapter of Revelation and examine Rev. 3.21: 'He who conquers, I will grant him to sit with me on my throne, as I myself conquered and sat down with my Father on his throne.' Here again we have a pericope associated in some fashion with a synoptic tradition extant in more than one version. In this case it is the Matthean passage which refers to the Son of Man and the Lucan which does not.

Truly, I say to you, in the new world, when the Son of Man shall sit on the throne of his glory, you who have followed me will also sit on twelve thrones, judging the twelve tribes of Israel. (Matt. 19.28)	You are those who have continued with me in my trials; as my Father appointed a kingdom for me, so do I appoint for you, that you may eat and drink at my table in my kingdom, and sit on thrones judging the twelve tribes of Israel. (Luke 22.28–30)

We hold that it is Matthew who represents the more primitive tradition,[13] while, in any event, it is the Matthean version with which Rev. 3.21b is most nearly associated.[14] This is most evident in the shared image of the eschatological hero sitting on God's own throne, an idea which is not part of the mainstream of Christianity[15] but which was known in several royal mythologies and surfaces again with the same Semitic phrase 'throne of his glory' in connection with the Son of Man in I Enoch.[16] This would strongly

[13] See above, pp. 26f.

[14] One notices the reference to those who 'eat with him' in Rev. 3.20 and wonders if there could also be some awareness of the form of tradition found in Luke. It could also be that the Matthean tradition has omitted such a conception, found as well in I Enoch 62.14 in association with the Son of Man. Cf. *SMMH*, 358 n. 4.

[15] More often he is pictured as sitting at God's right hand. (A similar conception, however, is not totally foreign to Revelation with its background in Jewish apocalyptic; cf. Rev. 5.6; 7.17; 22.3.) The ideogram of the followers sharing in the rule of the eschatological hero, on the other hand, becomes more common; e.g. Rev. 20.4; II Tim. 2.12.

[16] Probably this understanding lies behind the picture in Dan. 7.9–14 as well. See *SMMH*, 141ff.

suggest that Rev. 3.21b is not only secondary but that somehow in
the course of its transmission and alteration a direct reference to
the Son of Man has been replaced.[17]

Finally, in the canonical New Testament, we should notice
I Tim. 2.5f.: 'For there is one God, and there is one mediator
between God and men, the man Christ Jesus, who gave himself a
ransom for all' (ὁ δοὺς ἑαυτὸν ἀντίλυτρον ὑπὲρ πάντων). This is to be
compared with Mark 10.45b (= Matt. 20.28b) which is there
predicated of the Son of Man: '. . . and to give his life as a ransom
for many' (καὶ δοῦναι τὴν ψυχὴν αὐτοῦ λύτρον ἀντὶ πολλῶν). It is far
from certain that there is a direct relationship between these verses.
They may owe their similarity to a common dependence on the
thought of Isa. 53 and/or a Christian soteriological tradition which
may or may not be dependent on Isaiah. The reference to 'man' in
I Tim. 2.5 could result from the preceding word ἀνθρώπων and the
need to disclose the nature of one who could act as a mediator. If,
however, the author of I Timothy does have some direct awareness of the tradition found in Mark 10.45b, then it is fairly certain
that the former is 'a Hellenistic rewriting of the original Semitic
form in Mark'.[18]

2. THE EARLY FATHERS

In all of the literature of the so-called Apostolic Fathers the Son of
Man designation is found on but one or two occasions. There are
no other references to the figure in I and II *Clement*, the *Didache*,
the *Epistle of Barnabas*, the *Letters* of Ignatius and Polycarp, the
Martyrdom of Polycarp, the *Shepherd of Hermas* or the fragments of
Papias. (For that matter, this is also true of the extant work of
later figures such as Aristides, Athenagoras, Theophilus, Melito
and Tatian, of course omitting the Diatessaron.)[19] This catalogue

---

[17] It is interesting that R. H. Charles (*The Revelation of St John* I, 102)
regarded both v. 5 and v. 21 as later additions by the author, perhaps further
suggesting that he may have adapted them from tradition in circulation.

[18] Higgins, *Jesus and the Son of Man*, 44, rightly citing as Semitic 'the Son of
Man', 'give his *soul*' and 'for many'. Cf. also above, pp. 23ff.

[19] Yet it is of some interest that in three situations in which Tatian seemingly had a straightforward opportunity to choose between the Son of Man
and 'I' (or 'he' = Jesus) in rival parallel sayings, he apparently selected the
direct reference to Jesus. (We cannot, of course, have any certain knowledge
regarding Tatian's own wording or the precise nature or number of the
sources from which he was working. Here we have reference to the transla-

of absent references includes as well a lack of quotation or allusion (with the title) to all gospel Son of Man logia and Dan. 7.13f. By contrast, the designations of Jesus as Christ (or Messiah) Son of God, Lord, Saviour or Logos are, comparatively speaking, frequent in this literature.

The one reference in the *Epistle of Barnabas* and the other in Ignatius's *Letter to the Ephesians* show no recognizable connection with Son of Man traditions from the Gospels. *Barnabas* 12.10a reads: 'Notice again, Jesus, not as son of man but as Son of God (οὐχὶ υἱὸς ἀνθρώπου ἀλλὰ υἱὸς τοῦ θεοῦ), by a type manifested in flesh.' This verse occurs in the course of a typological exercise showing how Jesus' victory over God's enemies was prefigured by God's promise recited through Moses to Joshua, son of Nun ('Ἰησοῦ, υἱῷ Ναυή),[20] to destroy Amalek. In these circumstances and due to the anarthrous usage of the expression, Barnabas is probably only emphasizing his understanding that Jesus, unlike Joshua, is the son of no mortal man, but rather the Son of God. We could feasibly translate quite legitimately, '. . . Jesus, not as a son of man, but as Son of God . . .' It is conceivable, however, that the author is alluding to the title found in the Gospels. Yet, if this be so, both by form and meaning, we are a good distance from the use of the expression in the Gospels, for even the references there to the Son of Man's lowliness were not concerned with emphasizing his human origin in this fashion.[21]

---

tion of one of the Arabic versions by H. W. Hogg in *The Ante-Nicene Fathers*, vol. IX, New York 1896, 43ff., while consulting other versions and fragments. For bibliography see J. Quasten, *Patrology*, vol. I, Westminster, Maryland 1950, 225ff., to which add L. Leloir [ed.] *Saint Éphrem, Commentaire de l'Évangile Concordant: Texte syriaque* [Manuscrit Chester Beatty 709], Dublin 1963.) See Diatessaron 8.35; 13.18f.; 23.40f. employing Matt. 5.11 versus Luke 6.22 (where the reference to 'exclusion' seems to show knowledge of Luke's wording; though here D. Plooij's edition of *The Liège Diatessaron*, Amsterdam, 1929–35, at 12ᵛ, 10, does contain a reference to the Son of Man); Matt. 10.32 versus Luke 12.8 and Matt. 16.21 versus Mark 8.31 (where mention of 'rejection' seems to show awareness of Mark's or Luke's text). These could, however, be regarded primarily as signs of preference for Matthew's text.

[20] The ancient Latin version reads 'son of Naue' also in v. 10a in lieu of 'son of man', but this is almost surely an error due to this reading in vv. 8 and 9.

[21] It, of course, also has a quite different meaning from the anarthrous form in Rev. 1.13; 14.14.

The reference in Ignatius's *Ephesians* 20.2 reveals a much more deliberate and certain theological intent, though the meaning given to the designation is at least as close to that found in *Barnabas* as to its valuation according to the evangelists. Speaking of the need for obedience and unity, Ignatius hopes that all will join 'in one faith and in Jesus Christ who, according to the flesh, was of the family of David, son of man, and Son of God' (τῷ υἱῷ ἀνθρώπου καὶ υἱῷ θεοῦ). Ignatius seems to be making use here of Paul's phraseology (though both may have been dependent on a form of confession in more general usage) in Rom. 1.3f., where Jesus is said to be 'of the lineage of David according to the flesh, designated Son of God in power according to the Spirit of holiness by his resurrection'.[22] Ignatius employs the expression in a manner which could well indicate a conscious reference to the occurrence of the title in the Gospels, but once more the usage shows no form of contact with any of the themes of the Gospel logia. If there is indication of any manner of Christian tradition here,[23] the points of reference would be with *Barnabas* 12.10 (just possibly Heb. 2.6 with its dependence upon Ps. 8.4) leading on to Irenaeus in *Against Heresies* V.21.3, etc.[24]

Of considerable further interest are some passages in this body of literature which do *not* make direct reference to the Son of Man. Our attention fastens especially on the fervently eschatological conclusion of the *Didache*, ch. 16. In v. 1 we find what appears to be an echoing and conflating of several closely allied synoptic or 'synoptic-like' (see below) pericopes: 'Watch (cf. Matt. 24.42; 25.13; Mark 13.35, 37) over your life; do not let your lamps be extinguished nor your loins ungirded (Luke 12.35). But be ready (Luke 12.40 = Matt. 24.44), for you do not know (Mark 13.33, 35; Matt. 25.13; 24.42) the hour (Luke 12.40 = Matt. 24.44; cf. Mark 13.32 = Matt. 24.36; Matt. 24.50; 25.13) when our Lord is coming' (Matt. 24.42: *your* Lord is coming). We are dealing here

[22] If Ignatius was using Paul, it is understandable that he might have wished to drop some of the language very susceptible to an adoptionistic interpretation.

[23] It is possible that Ignatius' reference to the 'new man Jesus Christ' (perhaps again a borrowing from the Pauline corpus, Eph. 2.15) in 20.1 made him think in terms of Jesus as 'son of man'.

[24] See also below, p. 86, on 'On the Resurrection', 44.23, and perhaps, in addition, p. 41 below on the Georgian version of the closing verses of the *Didache*. Compare also (pp. 74f. below) the form of address for Jesus used by the gnostic Justin in Hippolytus, *Refut.* V.26.30.

with very complex 'synoptic' traditions which seem to have become interwoven and confused even in the Gospels themselves. Originally these were probably fragments from parabolic materials which spoke both of the sudden and unexpected return of a householder (and there appear to be several versions of that story) and of the sudden coming of a thief. Sometimes this unexpected time was spoken of as a *day*, sometimes as an *hour*. Since we also find several synoptic sayings (see references above) in which day and hour are combined, it is likely that at a later stage in the tradition the two means of stating this motif become interchangeable.

We have otherwise suggested that the understanding of the figure who is suddenly *coming* as the Son of Man (so a series of gospel passages) belongs to much older material and, if not an influence upon the message preached by Jesus, was at least an influence in quite primitive traditions.[25] The formulation which tells of the *Lord*[26] coming is later and perhaps derives out of the expression ὁ κύριος τῆς οἰκίας (Mark 13.35) and/or ὁ κύριος τοῦ δούλου (Matt. 24.50).

Now, a detailed comparison makes it quite clear that, if the *Didache*'s author was actually making use of one or more of our Gospels, he then knew sayings which spoke of the Lord coming and also which told of the coming of the Son of Man. In this event, he has selected the phraseology of the former. If, on the other hand, he was instead making use of extant oral tradition at this point or some other form of tradition (Christian or Jewish), it would seem either that he again knew both comparisons and chose to speak of the Lord rather than the Son of Man, or that it was the secondary tradition which alone had been passed on to him. In the latter instance, we might glimpse a yet earlier stage in which some Christians preferred to speak of Jesus *coming* as the Lord rather than as the Son of Man.

[25] Köster offers a detailed argument suggesting that *Did.* 16 is based, not on material borrowed directly from the synoptic Gospels, but rather on that which in origin was a Jewish apocalypse which also was used in Mark 13 and which influenced other synoptic materials. See *Synoptische Überlieferung bei den apostolischen Vätern*, 173–90. In this event, however, the absence of the Son of Man designation would, for our purposes here, be equally if not more significant, as Köster does not doubt that the designation was to be found in the earlier source.

[26] Köster (*op. cit.*, 90) suggests that the substitution of 'Lord' for 'Son of Man' is a specific sign of later Christianization of a Jewish work or of a Jewish-Christian writing now being further Christianized.

Something of a similar process is seen again in vv. 6–8 of this same sixteenth chapter of the *Didache*:

(6) And then will appear the signs of the truth. First the sign spread out[27] in heaven, then the sign of a sound of a trumpet and, in the third place, the resurrection of the dead. (7) (Yet not of all the dead, but as it was said, 'The Lord will come and all his saints with him' [Zech. 14.5].) (8) Then will the world see the Lord coming on[28] the clouds of heaven.

We should here compare Matt. 24.30f.:

(30) Then will appear the sign of the Son of Man in heaven, and then all the tribes of the earth will mourn, and they will see the Son of Man coming on the clouds of heaven with power and great glory; (31) and he will send out his angels with a loud trumpet call, and they will gather his elect from the four winds, from one end of heaven to the other.

Once again we are dealing with a complex tradition[29] which has possibly been penetrated by language from I Thess. 4.16 and certainly by Zech. 14.5b. There may, in addition, be some association with Rev. 1.7 (or its tradition) which also, we recall, made use of Matt. 24.30f. (or a tradition like it), but without employing the Son of Man designation. Here it would seem likely that the interruption by the Zechariah reference could have caused the omission of the Son of Man, Jesus having been identified with 'the Lord' of the quotation.[30] This may have been accomplished by the

---

[27] It is possible that this should be interpreted as the sign of the spreading out of the heavens, i.e. their opening. (Even in this event, however, it still seems that the author has a tradition like Matt. 24.30 in mind due to the linking of 'sign', 'trumpet' and the language of v. 8.) Perhaps the sign of the Son of Man has been interpreted in the light of a tradition like John 1.51: '. . . you will see the heaven opened, and the angels of God ascending and descending upon the Son of Man.'

[28] ἐπάνω. See below on Justin Martyr's wording.

[29] Köster's view (*op. cit.*, 185–90) of these verses is again integrated with his understanding of the formation of all of *Did.* 16. In these terms v. 6 is not based upon Matt. 24.30f., but rather do both make use of the language of Jewish and/or Jewish-Christian apocalyptic tradition. It is in these terms (see above, pp. 31f.) that Rev. 1.7 need also not be dependent upon Matt. 24.30f. Significant for our purposes is the awareness that Matt. 24.30f. mentions the Son of Man and that Rev. 1.7 and *Did.* 16.6 incorporate or are immediately followed by phraseology which was originally (so also Köster) associated with the Son of Man. It is strongly suggested, therefore, that one or more lines of tradition were moving in the direction of dropping this title.

[30] Zech. 14.5 speaks of 'the Lord your (or *my*) God'. This reference, too, has apparently been altered to facilitate the new understanding. Köster again

author or by earlier tradition. While it is impossible to date the *Didache* or its sources with any precision, we know that parts of it reach back into older material,[31] and it could be that the process we have glimpsed in *Didache* 16 reflects an early way of dealing with the tradition.

It should also be noted, however, that the ending of the *Didache* given above as conveyed by the Bryennios manuscript (Codex Hierosolymitanus) may well be incomplete[32] and could be supplemented according to the sense of the fuller endings found in the seventh book of the Greek *Apostolic Constitutions* or in the Georgian Version. In the *Constitutions* (omitting the final 'of heaven') there is added:

. . . with the angels of his power upon a kingly throne, to judge the world-deceiver, the devil, and to repay each according to his deeds. Then the wicked will depart to eternal punishment, but the righteous will enter life eternal . . .

There is evidently a reminiscence of the parable of the sheep and goats here (cf. Matt. 25.31ff.: with the Son of Man sitting on his throne accompanied by angels) and probably of Matt. 16.27 (another Son of Man logion) as well.

The Georgian version closes in the following manner:

Then will the world see our Lord Jesus Christ, the Son of Man[33] who (at the same time) is Son of God, coming on clouds with power and dominion [see Mark 13.26] and in his holy righteousness to repay every man according to his deeds before all men and angels. Amen.

There are enough common denominators here at least to suggest that the *Didache* once ended with further references to language elsewhere associated with the Son of Man. The Georgian version, of course, makes this subject explicit, but this is probably quite secondary, as it is not found in the other versions, and the translator

---

suggests that *Did.* 16.8 is dependent on Jewish apocalyptic language independently employed by its author and Mark (now more primitively reflected in Mark 14.62 than in the present version of Mark 13.26) which originally spoke of the Son of Man.

[31] See R. A. Kraft, *Barnabas and the Didache*, New York 1965 (Vol. III of *The Apostolic Fathers*, ed. R. M. Grant), 57–77.

[32] See P. Vielhauer in Hennecke's *New Testament Apocrypha* (= *NTA*, ed. W. Schneemelcher), ET, ed. R. McL. Wilson, London 1963–5, Vol. II, 628.

[33] Cf. above, p. 38 n. 24.

seems to have built upon the title 'Lord' already present and then compounded several Christological designations. His sensibilities were correct, however; much Son of Man language was used throughout *Didache* 16, though without the use of the title.

We can also recognize several somewhat more subtle illustrations of this tendency not to use the Son of Man designation in II *Clement*. In 2.4 the author quotes Matt. 9.13 parr.: 'I did not come to call the righteous but sinners.' This he glosses (v. 5): 'This means that he must save the perishing.' He continues in v. 7: 'So Christ also willed to save the perishing (σῶσαι τὰ ἀπολλύμενα), and he saved (ἔσωσεν) many, coming (ἐλθών) and calling us who were already perishing (ἀπολλυμένους).' There appears to be present here a reminiscence of a tradition like Luke 19.10: 'For the Son of Man came (ἦλθεν) to seek and to save the lost (σῶσαι τὸ ἀπολωλός).'[34] In rather typical fashion, however, the author has allowed his reminiscence to be influenced by language from elsewhere in the New Testament, seemingly in this case by Matt. 9.13 and by Pauline references (I Cor. 1.18; II Cor. 2.15; 4.3; II Thess. 2.10; see also II *Clem.* 1.4) to those 'perishing'. In the process the Son of Man has once again either been replaced, or, if one concludes that the author is only making a more generalized usage of what had become characteristic Christian language, he has not used the opportunity to refer to the Son of Man figure.

In II *Clem.* 3.2 the author quotes a logion which in the version of Luke 12.8 makes reference to the Son of Man, but he employs the rival parallel rendering found in Matt. 12.32 in which Jesus speaks directly of himself in the first person.[35] In II *Clem.* 11.6 the author may allude to Matt. 16.27.[36] He at least passes over a chance to refer to the Son of Man. The reference in II *Clem.* 12.1 to waiting while not knowing the day of the appearance of God reminds us once more of the absence in these writings of phrases

[34] Versions of the saying apparently had some popularity as additions to the text in Luke 9.56 and Matt. 18.11 show. Accordingly it may have been out of some other line of tradition than Luke 19.10 that this writer quoted.

[35] Köster (*op. cit.*, 71–73) holds that the author is, in effect, making direct use of Matthew's Gospel. Interestingly the author has now lost the Aramaism (see also above, pp. 33f., on Rev. 3.5b) ὁμολογεῖν ἐν.

[36] The idea of rendering to each man according to his works is, however, a commonplace. See Ps. 62.12; Rev. 2.23; 22.12, and Köster, *op. cit.*, 107. While II *Clement* uses language like that of Matt. 16.27, the wording stands even closer to Rom. 2.6.

traditional in the Gospels regarding the day, hour and parousia of the Son of Man.

The picture we have been sketching to this point is altered to a degree when we come to Justin Martyr. His references to the Son of Man can usefully be divided into two categories. There are those which employ or depend directly upon Dan. 7.13 and others involved with a version of one of the Son of Man passion predictions. In the *First Apology* 51.9, toward the end of a long disquisition on Old Testament prophecy and its powers to foretell the coming of Christ, his suffering, death, resurrection and ascension, Justin writes: 'And hear what the prophet Jeremiah said regarding how he was to come again from heaven in glory. Here are his words: "Behold as Son of Man he comes upon the clouds of heaven and his angels with him." ' This, of course, is not a direct quotation from the LXX or from any other known version of Daniel. Justin is probably quoting from memory, rather than from the text or from a collection of Old Testament testimonia, as his apparent error[37] with regard to the source would also indicate. Influence of the synoptic tradition is probably shown by the conception of the angels coming with him[38] and perhaps the idea of his appearing *on* (ἐπάνω) the clouds.[39] There are, however, no precise parallels to this version in the Gospels, and Justin's indebtedness to Daniel is probably indicated by his anarthrous use of the term. Indeed, wherever Justin refers to the hero of Daniel's prophecy, and on the two occasions when he goes on to explicate the title, he does so in terms of ὡς υἱὸς ἀνθρώπου, but when quoting from the Gospels he speaks of the figure as ὁ υἱὸς τοῦ ἀνθρώπου.

That Justin knew and could refer to the source of his quotation

---

[37] Justin may, however, be expressing himself rather imprecisely at this juncture and have simply left out a step which would have referred the specific quotation to Daniel. Yet see below, p. 48, on a similar misstatement regarding Hosea and Zechariah.

[38] Cf. Mark 13.27 (= Matt. 24.31); Mark 8.38 = Luke 9.26 with Matt. 16.27; Matt. 13.41; 25.31. See also below *Dial.* 31.1; 79.2. It could also be that both Justin and/or the synoptics derive the conception of the accompanying angels from those versions of Daniel which speak of οἱ παρεστηκότες.

[39] See Matt. 24.30; 26.64. Outside Justin (see *Dial.* 14.8; 31.1; cf. 120.4) there appears to be only one other use of this particular word in connection with the Son of Man's nebular appearance, *Did.* 16.8. (When Justin quotes more fully from the text of Daniel in *Dial.* 31.3, he speaks more traditionally: μετὰ τῶν νεφελῶν.) The nuances of the word might even suggest *above* or *over* and could conceivably point to some line of interpretation and usage of the Danielic language.

is made evident in the *Dialogue with Trypho* 31.3. There he makes copious use of Daniel 7 and, while his version is not a precise presentation of any known Greek translation, the quotation of Dan. 7.13 is sufficiently accurate. His indifference to exact quotation, however, and his probable dependence upon his own conception (influenced by the synoptics) of this great advent is seen in *Dial.* 31.1, introducing the long quotation. After contrasting the glory to come with Christ's previous suffering, he writes: 'For as Son of Man will he come upon (ἐπάνω) clouds, as Daniel indicated, angels accompanying him.' The probability of dependence upon memory rather than some form of written or fixed oral tradition is seemingly strengthened by the several differences between this presentation and that in I *Apol.* 51.9. Here we read: ὡς υἱὸς γὰρ ἀνθρώπου ἐπάνω νεφελῶν ἐλεύσεται . . . ἀγγέλων σὺν αὐτῷ ἀφικνουμένων. There we find: ἰδοὺ ὡς υἱὸς ἀνθρώπου ἔρχεται ἐπάνω τῶν νεφελῶν τοῦ οὐρανοῦ καὶ οἱ ἄγγελοι αὐτοῦ σὺν αὐτῷ. While the same basic ideas are present in roughly the same order, there are a number of obvious variations in the wording.

At the beginning of the next chapter (*Dial.* 32.1) Trypho (we may sympathize with him just having had twenty consecutive verses of scripture quoted at him) is said to have picked up the challenge of the Daniel quotation by means of reference to that familiar stumbling-block in Jewish versus Christian controversy: how should the Christ suffer? He here speaks of 'that glorious and great Messiah who, as Son of Man, receives the everlasting kingdom from the Ancient of Days'. It is obvious that Trypho, we are to assume,[40] as well as Justin, equated the figure in Daniel with the conception of the Christ, as it is also clear that the language here is borrowed from the preceding quotation. But, as Justin does no more with the equation and allusion, this is evidently language used here essentially as little more than a bridge to more 'proofs' that Jesus is the *Christ*.

On three more occasions in his *Dialogue* Justin speaks of the Danielic Son of Man. Since it is a basic intention of this treatise to demonstrate that Jewish scripture is a witness to the coming of

---

[40] After I Enoch 46ff. Jewish references, which might be traced to this period, to the figure of Dan. 7.13 as a messianic type are, however, rare, some suggest as the result of the Christian adaptation of the figure. With reference especially to b. Sanh. 97a (compare also 98a) and Tanchuma B. Toldoth 20 (70b) cf. H.-J. Schoeps, *Paul: The Theology of the Apostle in the Light of Jewish Religious History*, ET, London 1961, 94.

Jesus as the Christ, this is not surprising. In 76.1 Justin maintains the view that Daniel was alluding to one who would receive the eternal kingdom and who would also become man while yet not having been born of human seed when he wrote 'as Son of Man'. In ch. 79, after Justin has just completed a tendentious interpretation of several prophetic passages in relation to the Matthean birth narrative, Trypho, we are told, while yet retaining a great reverence for the scriptures, was angered by Justin's arguments, claiming them to be artificial. Wishing to hold his opponent's attention, Justin retorts in a milder fashion: 'Sir, I respect your piety, and I pray that you may feel the same way toward him whom the angels are said to serve, as Daniel says, "One as Son of Man is led to the Ancient of Days, and all dominion is given to him forever and ever." '[41] Finally, in *Dial.* 126.1, in a list of many names given to Christ in Old Testament prophecy, Justin includes among them, 'as Son of Man by Daniel'.

Justin's other source for reference to the Son of Man is evidently the passion saying found in Mark 8.31 and its closest parallel, Luke 9.22. On the first two occasions (*Dial.* 51.2; 76.7) the essential purpose is apparently to show that Christ himself was a prophet who, having himself been foreseen in scripture, realized this in his own prophecy. In the third instance (*Dial.* 100.3) the quotation is also produced as a proof that Jesus was able to interpret his own destiny, specifically with his liability to suffering in mind.

The quotations compare to or differ from the Mark 8.31 = Luke 9.22 tradition in the following ways (but see further below on variations peculiar to *Dial.* 51.2):

(*a*) In each case Justin reads σταυρωθῆναι in lieu of the Gospels' ἀποκτανθῆναι. This more definitive motif is, however, found as a substitute in the Son of Man passion saying Matt. 20.19f. and in both a Matthean and a Lucan formulation of a Son of Man saying, Matt. 26.2; Luke 24.7. Justin, probably influenced by this later understanding or by a later form of tradition built upon it, has used 'be crucified' here. Obviously it provides a more satisfactory

---

[41] Again the version differs from Justin's own quotation of Dan. 7 and is apparently an abridgment from memory. More interesting is the reference to the angels who serve him. Yet, since there seems to be no indication of a fixed formula here which would suggest a line of tradition or quotation from some *testimonia*, one surmises that this reference harks back to *Dial.* 31.1 and the angels who *accompany* him, the conception depending ultimately on reminiscences of synoptic tradition and/or οἱ παρεστηκότες as in *Dial.* 31.3.

rendering, especially when Jesus' powers for prediction are being emphasized.

(b) Justin speaks of Jesus' persecutors as 'scribes and Pharisees' (reversed in 100.3). While this combination is found in none of the Son of Man passion sayings ('elders, chief priests and scribes' are mentioned in Mark 8.31 parr.), it became a stock phrase in Christian tradition and would easily have been substituted.

(c) Justin's versions follow Luke (and Matthew) in reading τῇ τρίτῃ ἡμέρᾳ rather than μετὰ τρεῖς ἡμέρας. This preference for *precision* is understandable.

(d) Justin's version has the Marcan ἀναστῆναι rather than the Lucan (and Matthean) ἐγερθῆναι.

On our view, Justin's language could readily be explained by assuming that he is quoting the Gospels out of a fixed tradition, built upon Mark, but preferring the phraseology noted in (a), (b) and (c) above for readily explicable reasons.[42] With the whole of Justin's use of Gospel sayings in view, one could agree with Arthur Bellinzoni that Justin may have 'used an extracanonical source later than our synoptic gospels'.[43] Probably this depends upon a *school* tradition which was at least well along the way toward forming a *written*[44] harmony of the synoptic Gospels.

It must be admitted, though, that the *Dial.* 51.2 version slightly complicates this picture. Bellinzoni may be a little quick to set it aside as 'not a direct quotation', since it differs from *Dial.* 76.7 and 100.3 by agreeing with Matt. 16.21 in speaking of 'he' instead of the Son of Man, in omitting καὶ ἀποδοκιμασθῆναι and thus also in following παθεῖν by ἀπό before listing the persecutors. There are, however, a number of other differences from the Matthean version, and otherwise Justin is in total agreement with the version supplied in *Dial.* 76.7; 100.3. The similarities with Matthew could also otherwise be accounted for: like Matthew, Justin has dropped καὶ ἀποδοκιμασθῆναι either because it seemed somewhat redundant or due to a lapse in memory. Luke 9.22 also introduces the per-

---

[42] A. J. Bellinzoni, *The Sayings of Jesus in the Writings of Justin Martyr*, suppl. to *NovTest* 17, Leiden 1967, 32, suggests that Justin's versions may be influenced by Luke 24.7 which does read τῇ τρίτῃ ἡμέρᾳ ἀναστῆναι. He also notes the occurrence of ἀναστῆναι in some texts of Luke 9.22.

[43] *Op. cit.*, 32. On 31 Bellinzoni lays the relevant sayings out in convenient parallel form.

[44] Cf. Bellinzoni, *op. cit.*, 140. The fixity with which these three quotations are given helps to substantiate this impression.

secutors with ἀπό and/or it may be the new conjunction with παθεῖν which (as in Matthew) occasioned the change of preposition. Finally, like Matthew,[45] in context Justin has found it more satisfying to refer to Jesus directly by a pronoun rather than by the Son of Man title.

If this be the correct view and Bellinzoni's general verdict still stands, then it is clear that Justin's use of this somewhat altered form of the Mark 8.31 tradition offers no evidence in itself which would indicate a significant history among his immediate predecessors of employing the Son of Man passion materials for apologetic or other purposes. Rather, in these two or three instances and primarily in order to show that Jesus also possessed prophetic powers and was able to read his destined suffering in the pages of scripture, Justin had reference to one of the well-established Son of Man logia in a version borrowed from the canonical Gospels. In the absence of other witnesses, one could guess that Justin was almost alone in so using a Son of Man saying during this period.

We should also recognize that *Dial.* 51.2 is not the only passage in which Justin might well have used the Son of Man designation but did not. *Dial.* 49 is devoted to a discussion of the relationship between Elijah, John and the Christ, while the Gospels several times view this association with respect to the Son of Man in lieu of Christ.[46] In 49.5 Justin makes explicit use of Matt. 17.11–13 while, however, omitting the mention of the Son of Man in 17.9 and 17.12b.

While it may be argued that Justin in *Dial.* 107.1 was quoting Matt. 16.4, a parallel logion without the Son of Man, rather than Matt. 12.39, which is followed by a Son of Man statement, it is also perfectly clear that he was making reference to the themes of Matt. 12.40 when he speaks of resurrection on the third day. But he does not mention that Son of Man whose type Matthew and Luke claim Jonah to have been.

In *Dial.* 120.4 Justin speaks of 'the object of our expectation', the one who is 'to come again upon (ἐπάνω) the clouds, even Jesus . . .' In I *Apol.* 52.1 the author claims that the prophets foretold two comings (παρουσίας): 'the one which already took place was that of a dishonoured and suffering man; the other will

---

[45] Cf. *SMMH*, 379.
[46] Cf. *SMMH*, 372ff.

take place, as it is predicted, when with glory he shall come from heaven, attended by his angelic host.' Later in the chapter Justin applies the language of Zech. 12.11f. to the figure, as does Matt. 24.30 when speaking of the Son of Man. Justin had, we remember, employed the title at the end of the previous chapter while referring to Daniel, and one could understand it throughout ch. 52, but he seems strangely reluctant to repeat it, as though it were not part of his common parlance. Similarly in *Dial.* 14.8 we read:

. . . some (prophetic words) have been spoken with reference to the first coming (παρουσία) of Christ, in which he is described as about to appear as without honour, without form and mortal; others speak of his second coming (παρουσία) when in glory and upon (ἐπάνω) the clouds he will appear, and your people will see and recognize him whom they pierced, as Hosea, one of the twelve prophets, and Daniel have predicted.

Again Justin is working with the familiar materials from Daniel and Zechariah. The probability that he is making allusions from memory is once more encouraged by his mistake with regard to source. Indeed, there is a kind of confessional pattern here which is repeated again and again[47] in other contexts and with other language by Justin. Jesus came first in human lowliness, as predicted, and will come again in glory. We remark, however, on his failure to use the Son of Man title, while other Christological titles abound, in such statements, even when employing language otherwise linked with the Son of Man.

One reason for this may be found when we examine the two passages in which Justin volunteers to explain the meaning of the title for Trypho. After using the Danielic reference in *Dial.* 76.1, he explains: 'For saying as Son of Man (ὡς υἱὸν ἀνθρώπου) means one that has become man and appears as such. But he would not be born of human seed.' Then in *Dial.* 100.3, having used *the* Son of (the) Man designation in a passion saying, Justin continues: 'He called himself Son of Man (υἱὸν οὖν ἀνθρώπου ἑαυτὸν ἔλεγεν) either because of his birth by a virgin who was, as I said, of the race of David and Jacob and Isaac and Abraham or because Adam himself was the father of these mentioned from whom Mary traces her descent.'

[47] Compare, for instance, *Dial.* 49.2, where once more Justin speaks of the two parousias of the Christ who, the second time, will come with glory and as judge of all.

The plain fact of the matter is that Justin was not sure what this title did mean. He thought it had something to do with Jesus' generation, but this, despite his attempted explanation in the first instance above, probably made it even more difficult to associate it with the language from Daniel when Justin used that language without making explicit reference to Dan. 7.13. On the evidence, Justin was not at ease with the designation and could not comprehend it so as to make good use of the numerous gospel logia predicated of the figure. Like many a Christian before and after him (and as the rest of *Dial.* 100 amply illustrates), Justin was far more accustomed to speak of Jesus as Christ and the Son of God. Though he several times refers to the one prophesied by Daniel and twice quotes a passion saying predicated of the Son of Man in order to help demonstrate the witness of scripture to Jesus and Jesus' own knowledge of God's plan for him, Justin is otherwise as unconcerned with the Son of Man title and as uncertain of its ranges of meaning as, from all appearances, were his near contemporaries. With the exception of the Mark 8.31 logion he avoids the Gospels' traditions predicated of the Son of Man, and, upon examination, his uses of the title reveal no contact with any continuing tradition which spoke of the Son of Man in worship or creed.

3. OTHER EARLY TRADITIONS

Perhaps the most interesting possibility with regard to some ongoing *orthodox* Christian tradition which spoke of the Son of Man is suggested by the common denominator between two otherwise disparate bits of early church tradition regarding the Son of Man. We are told that both Hegesippus and the Gospel according to the Hebrews reported incidents in which James, 'the Lord's brother', was associated with statements regarding the Son of Man. Of course, scholarly caution is demanded. There is so little information regarding the Son of Man in non-gnostic Christian circles, and even less which bears any real affinity to the Gospels' traditions, that two fragments of legend, which may only be associated by coincidence, can readily become a tendency, a tendency a line of tradition and then a whole *school* of the Christian heritage.[48] Still, coincidence or not, the materials are intriguing.

[48] The most interesting theory in this regard is that of H.-J. Schoeps, *Jewish Christianity: Factional Disputes in the Early Church*, ET, Philadelphia 1969,

Eusebius (*Eccl. Hist.* II.23.13), quoting from Hegesippus'
account of James' martyrdom, reports that just before his death
James called out in a loud voice: 'Why do you ask me concerning
the Son of Man? He is sitting in heaven on the right hand of the
great Power, and he will come on the clouds of heaven.' Excerpt-
ing, he maintains, from the Gospel according to the Hebrews,
Jerome reports as follows on events immediately subsequent to
the resurrection:

'But the Lord, after he had given his grave clothes to the servant of the
priest, appeared to James (for James had sworn that he would not eat
bread from that hour in which he drank the cup of the Lord until he
should see him rising again from among those that sleep).' And again, a
little later it says, ' "Bring a table and bread," said the Lord.' Immediately it is added: 'He brought bread and blessed and broke it and
gave to James the Just (*Iusto*) and said to him, "My brother, eat your

---

62ff. He maintains that 'the Ebionite Jewish Christians certainly confessed
Jesus as "the Son of man" ' (*op. cit.*, 62). He goes on to argue that their
Christology, which regarded Jesus as a man in whom an angelic being had
taken residence and who then was transformed at his exaltation into a kind
of supernatural angelic being, would fit well with a veneration of Jesus as the
Son of Man. It was their strongly millenarianist and apocalyptic views which
'finally rendered the title "Son of man" unusable by the church' (*op. cit.*, 63).
It should also be noted that, according to Schoeps, it can be taken as 'established fact' that Jesus viewed himself as the Son of Man (*op. cit.*, 7). Such
understandings could, no doubt, help to account for some of our evidence
and it is far from improbable that some sectarian group may have carried on
the earliest christological themes. It must also be said, however, that Schoeps's
case is very largely built on inference and is influenced by his own understandings concerning the importance of the Ebionite group. The only real
evidence on which the argument can be based results from the possibility
that the Ebionites did use that Gospel according to the Hebrews (see
Eusebius, *Eccl. Hist.* III.27) from which Jerome says he drew a passage which
refers to the Son of Man (see below). Even this evidence cannot, however, be
assessed with any certainty since the Gospel according to the Hebrews which
Epiphanius (*Pan.* XXX.3.7) says the Ebionites called their gospel does not
appear to be the same gospel from which other fragments of a Gospel according to the Hebrews are drawn. None of the early fathers speak of the Ebionites
worshipping the Son of Man, and, although one can maintain a connection
between the Ebionites and earlier materials underlying the pseudo-Clementine
literature (see below, pp. 75ff.), Schoeps must admit (*op. cit.*, 63) that the
Son of Man designation is not there employed in a manner which he could
directly associate with his understanding of the Ebionite usage. On the other
hand, it is true that the James who is vital to these two passages which refer
to the Son of Man was apparently venerated by the Ebionites, though it is also
true, as indicated below, that he was venerated by a number of other sectarians
as well.

bread, for the Son of Man (*filius hominis*) is risen from among those who sleep." '49

These passages help to confirm our awareness of the vital place which this James came to play in Christian traditions. Not only was a collection of teaching materials attributed to him and included in the New Testament canon, but he also was claimed as the author of a *protevangelium*[50] and his position of prominence is maintained in a number of Christian traditions among them the pseudo-Clementine writings. This general impression has been further strengthened by the discovery of three works at Nag Hammadi which are dependent upon special revelations given to James or which he himself reveals.[51] Undoubtedly the major catalyst here, more important even than James' position in the New Testament writings and his role as head of the Jerusalem church, is his relationship to Jesus. Although the traditions are often concerned to maintain that James was not the actual physical brother of Jesus (e.g. First Apocalypse of James, CG V/3, 24.15: not 'in the material' = ὕλη; Second Apocalypse of James, CG V/4, 50.23: 'milk brother'), he was regarded as being as closely related as any man could be. Legends naturally developed.

Hegesippus' account of James' martyrdom, as given by Eusebius, is clearly embroidered with such legendary elements. There is the reflection of a possibly sound tradition that he was stoned to death.[52] One wonders, however, about the picture of his being thrown down from the temple wall (although this, too, is mentioned in other literature),[53] and many other details in Hegesippus' narration are clearly derived from hagiography and not history.[54]

[49] *De viris illustribus* 2.
[50] Mary is the figure of central interest in this apocryphal work, the major purpose of which is to assure belief in her perpetual virginity. James is said to be the author in order to give the strongest possible support to this tradition.
[51] According to Hippolytus the Naassenes also traced their tradition through Mary Magdalene to James, the brother of the Lord.
[52] So Josephus (*Ant*. XX.200), though he dates this event some five or six years earlier in AD 62.
[53] So Clement of Alexandria in Eusebius, *Eccl. Hist*. II.1.5. See the account of the martyrdom in the Second Apocalypse of James, CG V, 60.28–63.30, on which cf. A. Böhlig, 'Zum Martyrium des Jakobus', in his *Mysterion und Wahrheit. Gesammelte Beiträge zur spätantiken Religionsgeschichte* (Arbeiten zur Geschichte des späteren Judentums und des Urchristentums VI), Leiden 1968, 112ff. Hegesippus' account is also found in Jerome, *de vir ill*. 2.
[54] The very name James the Just (δίκαιος), which he is given here and

In particular, we may notice that the statement about the Son of Man is not found in any other account of the martyrdom. We may with some safety, then, regard it as a second-century creation, though an important question remains: was it part of a tendency at some locale and time during this period to fashion Son of Man traditions?

We consider this to be unlikely and suggest rather that the outcry of James was essentially a literary formulation based on New Testament materials and created either by Hegesippus or the tradition before him for obvious hagiographical reasons. Like Jesus and Stephen preceding him, James, before his martyrdom (as in Stephen's case by stoning), makes his confession concerning the Son of Man in the face of an assembly in which many high Jewish officials are to be found. Like his predecessors, James also asks the Father to have mercy upon them 'for they know not what they do'.[55] The confession itself appears to be modelled closely upon Matt. 26.64 with its parallel Mark 14.62. Most significant is its retention of the periphrasis 'Power' ($\delta\acute{u}\nu\alpha\mu\iota s$) for God.[56] The introductory statement ('Why do you ask me concerning the Son of Man?') has probably only been formed in order to lead into the exclamation, though the previous question of the Jewish leaders ('Who' or 'What is the gate ($\theta\acute{u}\rho\alpha$) of Jesus?') remains a puzzle.[57]

Our view of *Eccl. Hist.* II.23.13 as a literary reminiscence appears to be corroborated by the surrounding testimony from Hegesippus's account. All the other material, both on the lips of

elsewhere (several times in the Nag Hammadi Apocalypses, e.g. CG V, 59.22) is evidently part of a second-century tradition, probably due to the rigour with which he was said to have clung to the Mosaic law. (Even the scribes and Pharisees, it is claimed, revered him and so addressed him. The title, of course, is also given to Jesus in Acts.) To later hagiography probably also belongs the description of him as a Nazirite.

[55] *Eccl. Hist.* II.23.16. So Luke 23.34. See Acts 7.60, and note that Stephen and James are both said to have been kneeling as they made their intercession.

[56] The reference to great Power ($\mu\epsilon\gamma\acute{a}\lambda\eta s$ $\delta\upsilon\nu\acute{a}\mu\epsilon\omega s$) may owe something to the reported language of Simon Magus. So Acts 8.10; Hippolytus, *Refut.* VI.9. 4.

[57] Gnostics speculated on the gate of life (perhaps influenced by Matt. 7.13 and/or John 10.9); e.g. the Naassenes linking it with speculation about the Primal Man (Hippolytus, *Refut.* V.8. 19f.), but it is difficult to find any helpful connection with the Naassenes and this passage. Possibly there is some link with the heavens opened in John 1.51; see *SMMH*, 278–80. Cf. Odes of Solomon 12.3.

James and his adversaries, uses Christ or other titles of Jesus,[58] but not Son of Man.

It is no less easy to conclude that Jerome's citation is a legendary accretion to tradition, though it is more difficult to ascertain the factors which occasioned its formulation. Grant and Freedman list some of the secondary characteristics.[59] There is the matter of this second-century title, James the Just. He is pictured as a guest at the Last Supper who there takes an oath similar to that of Jesus. The eclectic character of the narrative is likely also indicated by the introduction of the 'high priest's slave' from John 18.10. It is suggested that the Emmaus narrative (see especially Luke 24.30) may have strongly influenced the formation of the story here at hand. Most significant of all is the movement of James into absolute primacy among the apostles. He is the first witness to the Lord's resurrection as Jesus goes to appear to him. Grant and Freedman conclude: 'In general the sole purpose of this story is to strengthen the claims of the Church of Jerusalem at the expense of gentile Christians.'[60]

All this does not tell us, however, why the Son of Man title was employed. If the passage was indeed drawn from the Gospel according to the Hebrews,[61] and if this saying was part of that original Gospel,[62] it must have been formulated some time in the second century, most likely before AD 150. Yet, as far as can be told from the fragments remaining and any other indications, the Gospel according to the Hebrews had no proclivity for the Son of Man designation.[63] On the basis of our explanation of the Son of

[58] See especially *Eccl. Hist.* II.23.2: 'Our Lord and Saviour Jesus Christ is the Son of God.'

[59] *The Secret Sayings of Jesus*, 35f.

[60] *Op. cit.*, 36.

[61] On the many problems involved with the enigmatic traditions regarding this Gospel see P. Vielhauer in *NTA* I, 117–39, especially 126–36. On the possibility of errors by Jerome cf. the example given by Grant and Freedman, *op. cit.*, 36.

[62] Most often, at least, Jerome seems to have been citing from passages said to have been drawn from this Gospel by others.

[63] If, as Quispel and some others maintain, the Gospel of Thomas drew from the Gospel of the Hebrews, it evidently drew few Son of Man logia. Only log. 86 in Thomas speaks of the Son of Man and this is a close replica of a saying found in Matthew and Luke (see below, p. 83). Nor do we find any use of the Son of Man designation in fragments of reputed Gospels which have sometimes been associated with that according to the Hebrews; i.e. Nazarenes, Ebionites. On one usage in the gnostic Gospel of the Egyptians, see in the next chapter.

Man saying in *Eccl. Hist.* II.23.13 there is also now no reason to associate the two traditions which link James with a statement about the Son of Man.[64]

Our best guess is that the use of the title should be considered in the light of the overall intention of the passage. The author, wishing to show James' pre-eminence, has refashioned and borrowed from several Gospel traditions to accomplish his purpose. In order to increase the 'authentic ring' of that which is supposed to come from the earliest of the churches' traditions he has made use of that title which is deeply woven in those materials. Were the title no longer in use in the author's community and thus somewhat esoteric and archaic sounding, so much the better!

Casting our net yet further, we can draw into view a number of apocryphal books created by largely non-gnostic Christian communities. From these other materials, some of which may be thought to depend on traditions of the middle of the second century or earlier, we find but a very few uses of the Son of Man title. In the Acts of Peter (*Actus Vercellenses*, ch. 24) in a passage containing several prophecies with regard to Jesus, Dan. 7.13 is quoted.[65] No further reference, however, is made to the figure in these Acts.

A clear example of the manner in which the title seems to have been avoided is found in the opening chapter of the Apocalypse of Peter, a work which may go back to the early part of the second century.[66]

Many will come in my name saying, 'I am Christ.' Believe them not and draw not near to them. For the coming of the Son of God will not be manifest, but like the lightning which shines from the east to the west, so shall I come on the clouds of heaven with a great host in my glory; with my cross going before my face[67] will I come in my glory, with all

[64] There is also an interesting reference to the Son of Man's resurrection in the treatise 'On the Resurrection', CG I/3, 46.14–20 (see below, p. 88), but the language employed is otherwise different and further common denominators do not appear to be present.

[65] The quotation is not exact, but the author refers to his source as 'the prophet', and the form *sicut filium hominis* assures that he is drawing upon Daniel with little or no influence here from the Gospels' traditions except perhaps in the idea of '*upon* a cloud' (*super nubem*).

[66] The Apocalypse of Peter 4 refers to Ezek. 37, where the prophet is addressed 'Son of Man', but no application is made to Jesus.

[67] Compare the cross following in the Gospel of Peter 39. Probably we have here a reference to the sign of the Son of Man in Matt. 24.30, which

my saints, my angels,[68] when my Father will place a crown upon my head, that I may judge the living and the dead.

Quite clearly this tradition has made use of and built upon the language associated with the Son of Man in logia like Mark 13.26; Matt. 16.27; 24.27, 30; Luke 9.26. Just as obviously has the designation been omitted, and, in fact, supplanted by the title Son of God. Material borrowed from several of these sayings and apparently from Mark 14.62 as well is also found in Apocalypse of Peter 6, again without use of the title.

4. CONCLUDING REMARKS

We find it difficult to overstate the impression left by our survey. Out of what is a relatively large body of Christian literature which can be dated or, with some probability, traced, at least in part, to the middle of the second century or earlier we find astoundingly few uses of a title which tends to dominate in the synoptic Gospels and which is well represented in the Fourth Gospel. Though Jesus in these Gospels is reported to have spoken of himself almost solely with reference to this designation and employed it at crucial junctures in his ministry, the later New Testament writers, the early Fathers and bearers and creators of tradition seem almost wholly unconcerned with it. Out of numerous fragments of lost works, letters, homilies and apocryphal writings, from writings representing different dates, locales, backgrounds and forms of Christianity, the impression remains the same.

Apart from Justin the references to the figure could be counted on one's fingers and are outweighed by far by contexts in which the Son of Man designation is deliberately or unconsciously avoided. Even in Justin's case we have seen that the usage is far from widespread and reflects only his immediate purposes in proving that Jesus was the one predicted by Daniel and who himself also prophesied his destined end. Other writers we have studied may on rare occasion use the title for similar ends (usually

---

came to be interpreted as the cross (or which was originally intended as such). Cf. *SMMH*, 361 n. 3.

[68] 'My saints, my angels' could be a mistranslation by the Ethiopic translator or an interpretation based upon the phrase 'the holy angels'; cf. Mark 8.38 = Luke 9.26.

by alluding directly to Dan. 7.13 and then employing the Danielic anarthrous form of the designation instead of the form standardized in the Gospels) or for a literary reason or in order to make reference to the humanity of Jesus. Only in one case (outside Justin's direct quotations of Jesus from the Gospels) do we find a Son of Man saying put on the lips of Jesus, although the Gospels unanimously and unequivocally witness to the fact that Jesus alone was reported to have spoken of the figure. In this way too, therefore, later witnesses show little or no contact with the characteristics of the tradition of the Gospels.

Why, we ask, was this so? It has been suggested that the employment of the designation by strongly apocalyptic and millenarianist Christian sects might have rendered the title unusable by others.[69] Yet there is no sign of any polemic against such a usage, and one might still have expected to find it in such works as the *Epistle of Barnabas*, *Didache* 16, Visions 1–4 of the *Shepherd of Hermas*, II *Clement* and a number of apocryphal writings which reveal a strong eschatological and sometimes apocalyptic bent. Furthermore, one must wonder, how could the 'misuse' of such a venerable designation by a few have rendered the title so quickly unusable by so many others practising their faith in a number of different locales?

Nor can it be forgotten that the title is often found in other distinctive and highly significant contexts in the traditions of the canonical Gospels. Perhaps some of the sayings having reference to the lowliness or earthly ministry of the Son of Man (Matt. 8.20 par.; 11.19 par.; cf. also Matt. 12.32 par.) might have come to sound somewhat paradoxical to those accustomed to worshipping Jesus as the divine Lord. Yet many of the sayings having to do with the persecution of those who followed the Son of Man and their subsequent vindication along with the condemnation of others (Luke 6.22; 12.8f. par.; Mark 8.38) or with the Son of Man's authority (Mark 2.10 parr.; John 5.27) and redeeming work

[69] Cf. above, p. 49 n. 48, on the view of Schoeps. The evidence presented in the next chapter might also suggest that it was a use of the title by gnostics which caused *more orthodox* Christians to give up the use of the designation. This remains a possibility, but again there is little or no indication that gnostics were using the title in a polemical fashion or in a manner which other Christians would have found wholly unreasonable in itself, except to the degree (see below, pp. 109ff.) that it may have been associated with figures other than Jesus. Certainly the way in which the title was used by Irenaeus tends to militate against such theories.

(Mark 10.45 par.) and especially those logia foretelling or employed in connection with his passion might have seemed to have been useful in any number of later contexts. Even if the sayings themselves were not used, one would have thought that the designation might have occasionally clung to a mention of these themes. In these circumstances one can only guess that the title must soon have become so 'foreign' sounding and difficult to comprehend that, for most Christians and for all practical purposes, it ceased to have any viability during this period.

Nowhere, then, can we find any legitimate hints of a real movement or practice which could in any sense be traced back to a tendency to speak of Jesus as the Son of Man. There is no indication that he was confessed or worshipped as either the historical or the heroic and enthroned Son of Man. To some degree we may also suspect that this was true of the men who taught and passed on the tradition to the authors here under study. One, of course, cannot claim too much, as historical movements can rise, flourish and die in a relatively short space of time, and far from all the evidence has survived from this period, but, if various groups and individuals within the Christian communities did create some or all of the variety of Son of Man materials now preserved in all of the identifiable gospel sources, they did so in ways which left very few if any vestiges in the traditions of a *more orthodox* Christian variety passed on to us from the subsequent period.

III

THE SON OF MAN IN GNOSTIC LITERATURE

THE Son of Man designation occurs with much more frequency in second-century materials of a decidedly gnostic character than it does in Christian writings which do not appear to be under this gnostic influence.[1] We shall here set out the relevant passages for our study and make comment upon them as seems necessary. As we do this, there are several difficult questions which we wish to keep particularly in mind. Do the various pericopes seem at all related to one another and/or to other less gnostic uses of the term? In what ways might they be related to other Christian materials? Are there any indications here of a non-Christian employment of the Son of Man title? Might some of these references point back to yet earlier contexts of usage? After reviewing the materials with questions like these in mind, we may then attempt some tentative conclusions.

I. REFERENCES BY EARLY CHRISTIAN FATHERS
TO GNOSTIC USES

Scholars long ago recognized that the accounts of gnostic movements given by Irenaeus and Hippolytus indicated extensive interest in versions of an Anthropos figure. Sometimes in conjunction with this heavenly figure reference is also made to the Son of Man.

[1] It is, of course, not yet possible to date most of the Coptic gnostic documents with any precision. We would contend, however, as do most scholars, that these manuscripts, largely from the fourth and fifth centuries, are in many cases dependent upon writings which achieved their essential form during the second century, although changes were undoubtedly made at later times, especially in the process of translation. Since greater accuracy than this is possible in only a few cases, we shall usually content ourselves with the general view, substantiated by Irenaeus and Hippolytus, that the Son of Man title was in some use in certain branches of Gnosticism, certainly before the end of the second century and seemingly from yet earlier decades.

In his presentation of the errant views of Colorbasus and his followers Irenaeus discusses two somewhat variant understandings of the Anthropos both of which were relatively widespread in second-century Gnosticism.[2] In the first mentioned of these (which, however, may be secondary in terms of its development) we hear of Anthropos as one of the primary emanations of the Propator. This understanding of Anthropos as a part of the primary Ogdoad is characteristic of the developed Valentinian system.[3] There *he* is often regarded as the partner of Ecclesia in one of these first syzygies. Though others among the followers of Colorbasus[4] regarded the saviour as having been formed from out of *all* or from the ten aeons emanating from Logos and Zoe, some held him to have his being from the twelve aeons who were the offspring of the Anthropos and Ecclesia. 'And on this account he acknowledges himself Son of Man (υἰὸν ἀνθρώπου), as being a descendant of Anthropos.'[5] Still others maintain, however, that the Propator of all is himself to be regarded as Anthropos. 'Thus does the saviour call himself Son of Man' (υἰὸν ἀνθρώπου).

We find these passages, as we shall find many another, in what is obviously a cosmogonic context and evidently a Christian setting. Immediately also we are faced with difficult questions about the character and origin of such language. Should it be regarded as wholly Christian, or, since references to the Man alone are found elsewhere in non-Christian as well as Christian settings, might we here be viewing an example of a syncretistic mythology. In these terms, the conception of the Man might derive from extra-Christian thought, while the idea that one of his emanations or offspring might be called the Son of Man would result from a borrowing of the designation found in traditional Christian materials, this rapprochement made possible by the obvious coincidence of anthropomorphic language. Certainly the manner in which Colorbasus is said to make the identification readily suggests this possibility here.

Or, since Colorbasus is said to have made reference to a number of differing and seemingly well-developed theories about the origin of the saviour, and since in many another gnostic system

[2] On the Anthropos in gnostic lore cf. *SMMH*, ch. II, and H.-M. Schenke, *Der Gott* 'Mensch' *in der Gnosis*, Göttingen 1962.

[3] E.g. in Irenaeus, *Adv. Haer.* I.11.1.

[4] Irenaeus may at this point only be speaking of Valentinians generally.

[5] Irenaeus, *Adv. Haer.* I.12.4.

the two titles Man and Son of Man are linked, is he in this case also making use of an earlier mythological understanding? Might, then, both the titles be borrowed not from Christianity directly but from Jewish-gnostic or Jewish cosmogonic-anthropogonic or eschatological thought?

Marcus was another said to be a disciple of Valentinian who was familiar with some version of an Anthropos myth. In his view, as reported first by Irenaeus, the *man* (ἄνθρωπος) Jesus was formed after the likeness and form of that heavenly Anthropos, and afterwards he came to possess Anthropos himself as well as other of the aeons. Earlier we are told that the power which descended at Jesus' baptism 'was the seed of the Father, having in itself both the Father and the Son as well as that power of *Sigē* (σιγῆς) . . . this was that Spirit which spoke by the mouth of Jesus and confessed himself to be Son of Man (υἱὸν ἀνθρώπου) as well as being one[6] who revealed the Father, and who, having descended into Jesus, was made one with him'.[7]

A reading of these passages together with their context suggests that Marcus had access to an understanding similar to that known by Colorbasus's disciples. There was a heavenly Anthropos to be regarded either as the high God or as one of his principal emanations, forming a syzygy with Ecclesia. The saviour could be styled Son of Anthropos. Indeed, he is to such a degree the counterpart of the Man that he himself may be said to possess Anthropos.

We notice here especially the apparent dependence of the story of the counterpart Man's formation on the language of Gen. 1.26f. Also we shall want to remember that the general pattern of thought has been associated either by Marcus or his tradition with the legend of Jesus' baptism. If the latter was the case, we might wonder if there are relics here of some earlier understanding of this baptism.[8]

In his account of the teaching of an Ophitic group Irenaeus is

---

[6] While the text of Irenaeus suggests that it is the Spirit who reveals the Father, Hippolytus might seem to indicate that it was Jesus as the Son of Man who did this.

[7] Irenaeus, *Adv. Haer.* I.15.3, with the parallel account in Hippolytus, *Refut.* VI.46.4.

[8] See below on the Gospel of Philip, sayings 54 and 120, and in *SMMH*, 278ff.; 298; 365ff. on John 1.51; 6.27 and the synoptic narratives of the baptism which may also indicate associations of this rite with the Son of Man designation.

once more required to report on the Father of All styled as the First Man.

They also maintain that his Ennoia, going forth from him, produced a son and that this is the Son of Man (υἱὸν ἀνθρώπου), second Man. Below these again is the Holy Spirit, and under this superior spirit the elements were separated from each other – water, darkness, the abyss, chaos . . .[9]

Once more the mythologizing seems dependent upon Genesis, in this case especially upon Gen. 1.2.[10]

We are next told that both the Man and his son, delighting in the beauty of the woman-Spirit, have intercourse with her, bringing forth 'the third male whom they call Christ, the son of the first and second Man and of the Holy Spirit, the first woman'.[11] We shall come to other accounts, especially in the Gospel of Philip and the Epistle of Eugnostos, which suggest this pattern of Man, Son of Man and a second son (i.e. a third figure) who is seen as the saviour. Here, as with other such instances, we notice that the Son of Anthropos seems to be regarded entirely as a heavenly being.

This realization is apparently underlined by an ensuing story of the creation of the first earthly anthropos, a man of immense size who could merely writhe along the ground until the spirit of life is breathed into him, and who then chooses to give thanks, not to Ialdabaoth his maker, but to the First Man, the true source of spirit and life.[12] This earthly figure is not, however, styled *son* of Anthropos.

In the immediately preceding narrative we are presented with a rather comic scene, apparently well known in gnostic lore,[13] to which we shall need to return later in our study. Ialdabaoth, the *ignorant* creator god, the demiurge, who is a caricature of the God of the Old Testament, proclaims that he is God and that above him there is no other. His mother, Sophia, however, makes light of his claim: 'Do not lie, Ialdabaoth, for the Father of all is above

[9] *Adv. Haer.* I.30.1.
[10] Cf. Schenke, *Gott* 'Mensch', 81.
[11] *Adv. Haer.* I.30.1; cf. I.30.2.
[12] *Adv. Haer.* I.30.6.
[13] Irenaeus may have been borrowing from a version of the Apocryphon of John, from a source also used by that writing or from a writing which used some of the same sources as the Apocryphon. See below, pp. 101ff.

thee, the First Man, and Man, Son of Man' (*primus anthropos et anthropos filius anthropoi* = πρῶτος ἄνθρωπος [καὶ ἄνθρωπος] υἱὸς ἀνθρώπου).[14] Elsewhere, as we shall see, this part of the story often read to the effect: 'Man exists and the Son of Man.'

Further on in this same section of Irenaeus's work the Christ above is said to descend directly from the First Anthropos.[15] He comes down upon Jesus, who is then capable of working miracles and proclaiming the unknown Father. In addition, he now can confess himself to be *son* of the First Man (*filium primi hominis*).[16] Here in a specifically Christian context we again meet a kind of pre-Nestorian or Antiochene Christology making use of the language employed earlier. No longer is a son of the First Man only a heavenly figure and co-father of the Christ. Rather (in a somewhat confusing manner), as or along with the Christ, he might be seen to have descended upon the earthly Jesus.

We ask, without yet any sure means of answering our question, whether the use of the Son of Man designation among the Ophites should consistently be regarded as a borrowing from Christianity. Carsten Colpe believes that all gnostic uses of the title should be viewed in this way and employs these materials to illustrate his point.[17] He would note that, although the styling of the Father of All as Man can readily be regarded as a non-Christian characteristic, the Son of Man is otherwise best known in Christian literature. In the account from *Against Heresies* I.30.1, quoted above, the Man has an Ennoia, thought. Colpe sees this feminine Ennoia as being identified with the masculine Son of Man and suggests that we have here an anomaly which can best be resolved by realizing that the Son of Man has synthetically been added to the system.

It is not certain, however, that Irenaeus originally contended

---

[14] *Adv. Haer.* I.30.6.

[15] *Adv. Haer.* I.30.11.

[16] *Adv. Haer.* I.30.13.

[17] Cf. C. Colpe, 'New Testament and Gnostic Christology' in *Religions in Antiquity* (Essays in Memory of E. R. Goodenough, ed. J. Neusner, Studies in the History of Religion XIV), Leiden 1968, 227ff., especially 238f. See also R. Schnackenburg, *The Gospel according to John*, vol. I (Herder's Theological Commentary on the New Testament), ET, New York 1968, 541, and Schenke, *Gott 'Mensch'*, 154. A more open stance, though inclining in the same direction, is taken by R. McL. Wilson with specific reference to the Ophite Son of Man. See his book, *The Gnostic Problem. A Study of the Relations between Hellenistic Judaism and the Gnostic Heresies*, London 1958, 195.

that the Ophites held Ennoia to be the Son of Man.[18] The version of the Greek passed along to us for this section appears to be considerably abridged and the Latin versions vary, their syntax (not atypically) not being entirely clear, leading to different translations. If, however, we understand that the Ennoia, instead of becoming 'a son', produced a son who was called the Son of Man, this would eliminate the anomaly of having the female Ennoia become a male and would correspond to the pattern found regularly elsewhere in Gnosticism, where from a male and female principle another male results. Such is, in fact, the generative process which is observed later on in this same section when the Man and his Son beget from the Spirit a third male.

We should also point out, however, that the androgyneity of heavenly beings is a characteristic of much gnostic thought,[19] and such figures are often then given a female as well as a male name. This is true as well of the Son of Man in a setting in which Christian influences are at least not obvious, the context of the Epistle of Eugnostos.[20] In these terms it is conceivable that Irenaeus has correctly recorded an Ophite conception which they, in turn, had borrowed from other speculations.[21]

By way of additional argument, one could also ask, even if the linking of Ennoia and the Son of Man is viewed as a hybrid conception of the Ophites, whether it might not be better to regard the female emanation as the intruding element. As we shall see, the Man and the Son of Man are elsewhere often linked in gnostic statements, a number of which have a genuine claim on our attention as belonging to relatively early gnostic thought. (There was, after all, directly out of the Jewish background a familiar story of the God creating a man who frequently in later speculation was regarded as another heavenly being and could sometimes be called a son.)[22] One could, therefore, just as well contend that the

[18] We should, of course, also reckon with the possibility that Irenaeus had misunderstood the original intention of the Ophites.

[19] As it was also of Adam in rabbinic speculations, especially with regard to the 'male and female he created them' of Gen. 1.27; e.g. Gen. Rabba 8.1.

[20] CG III, 81.21ff., with parallel in CG V, 10.4ff. The passage is found in a similar form in the *Sophia Jesu Christi* (BG 8502) 102.15ff. and its parallel. On the relation of these two works, see below, pp. 94ff. Note also the hermaphrodite character of the son of the Son of Man in CG V, 13.12f.

[21] There was also an hermaphrodite conception of the Son of Man current among the Naassenes. See below, p. 73.

[22] On the role of Gen. 1.26f. in gnostic thought, see below, pp. 117ff.

standard gnostic idea of a female thought principle has here been intruded by the Ophites to help account for received information concerning the generation of a second (or 'Son of') Man.

We must also notice that the heavenly, cosmogonic Son of Man first presented here has little point of contact with the Son of Man found in canonical Christian literature. He is neither an eschatological judge nor an earthly sufferer or saviour, and thus a derivation from that Christian source is at least not obvious. Moreover, when we do come to specifically Christian Ophite material, and when the Christ above descends upon Jesus, although he then confesses himself to be '(the) Son of (the) First Man', the regular designation (i.e. Son of Man) is not there employed. One can at least wonder, therefore, whether these Ophites were not attempting to conform to their Christian ideas a conception received from another source, and thus whether they knew the Son of Man designation as a uniquely Christian term.

The Peratae, unlike most of the groups and writings we shall study, seem either not to have known or not to have been concerned to make use of the widely known Man conception. They also had marked Ophitic tendencies, were more strongly and obviously Christian than a number of other sects and, in this connection, apparently had direct knowledge of 'canonical' Christian writings. Especially do they make use of the Gospel of John. This employment of Christian 'scriptures' together with Irenaeus's lack of concern with the group might cause us to believe that they appeared as a relatively late sect on the second-century scene.

Hippolytus reports that the Peratae claimed that the Christ descended from the 'unorigination' above. The Peratic maintained that it was thus spoken, 'For the Son of Man (ὁ υἱὸς τοῦ ἀνθρώπου) did not come into the world to destroy the world, but that the world through him might be saved.'[23] Here, for the first time in our review of the gnostic Son of Man references, we find a statement which not only clearly relates to materials found in the canonical Gospels but which also employs the familiar articular form in the Greek. Colpe would emphasize the parallelism with John 3.17,[24] though it would also seem that a version of Luke 9.56a has played its role.

[23] Hippolytus, *Refut.* V.12.7.
[24] Colpe, *TWNT* VIII, 479. He suggests that Son of Man has been used here to substitute for Son of God.

John 3.17	Refut. V.12.7	Luke 9.56a
οὐ γὰρ	οὐ γὰρ	ὁ γὰρ
ἀπέστειλεν ὁ θεὸς	ἦλθεν	
τὸν υἱὸν	ὁ υἱὸς τοῦ ἀνθρώπου	υἱὸς τοῦ ἀνθρώπου
		οὐκ ἦλθεν
εἰς τὸν κόσμον	εἰς τὸν κόσμον	ψυχὰς (ἀνθρώπων)
ἵνα κρίνῃ	ἀπολέσαι	ἀπολέσαι
τὸν κόσμον	τὸν κόσμον	
ἀλλ' ἵνα σωθῇ	ἀλλ' ἵνα σωθῇ	ἀλλὰ σῶσαι
ὁ κόσμος δι' αὐτοῦ	ὁ κόσμος δι'αὐτοῦ	

It is evident that variants on a saying like Luke 9.56a circulated both outside and inside the orbit of synoptic tradition,[25] and one can therefore wonder whether this Peratic pericope ought best to be regarded as a tradition formed out of the written Gospels or as a saying which has, in one way or another, been influenced by oral tradition. Such an oral tradition could, of course, itself be based upon written materials, but there is at least a possibility that this saying current among the Peratae points back to some earlier context[26] in which the Son of Man designation had a more regular coinage. Indeed, it is not impossible, though hardly demonstrable, that all of these logia derive from some common archetype. In this case, one can only speculate as to whether 'Son' or 'Son of Man' or some other means of reference was first used in the saying as a designation for Jesus.

The knowledge among the Peratae of Johannine tradition is clearly indicated in *Refutation* V.16.11, where, in the midst of a discourse on the saving power of the serpent elevated by Moses in the wilderness, reference is made to the saying found at John 3.14: 'In the same manner as Moses lifted up the serpent in the wilderness, so must the Son of Man be lifted up.'

Refut. V.16.11	John 3.14
καὶ ὃν τρόπον	καὶ καθὼς
ὕψωσε Μωυσῆς	Μωυσῆς ὕψωσεν
τὸν ὄφιν ἐν τῇ ἐρήμῳ	τὸν ὄφιν ἐν τῇ ἐρήμῳ
οὕτως ὑψωθῆναι	οὕτως ὑψωθῆναι
δεῖ τὸν υἱὸν τοῦ ἀνθρώπου	δεῖ τὸν υἱὸν τοῦ ἀνθρώπου

[25] On Luke 9.56a together with Luke 19.10 and Matt. 18.11, cf. *SMMH*, 326f. The influence of some such logion, employing the title Christ, is apparently found also in II *Clem.* 2.7. See above, p. 42.

[26] On the context of this logion in Hippolytus and the relationship with another saying which may once have had reference to the Son of Man, see further below, pp. 66ff.

Probably it is wisest to assume that the Peratae have taken this quotation directly from the canonical Gospel known to us.[27] One is only given pause by the obvious recognition that the Peratae have given a context and a rationale to this Son of Man logion which is decidedly lacking in John's Gospel. On this basis one might again wonder if their use of the saying does not result from their contacts with Ophites or Naassenes and an older tradition which called for the use of the Son of Man designation on these terms.

There was also evidently current among the Peratae this saying: 'All the fullness was pleased to dwell in him bodily, and in him is all the divinity. . . .'[28] This statement is of interest to us because similar words were said to have been used by Monoïmus: '. . . that all the fullness was pleased to dwell on the Son of Man bodily'.[29] It might at first seem that the Peratae and Monoïmus were making obvious use of Col. 1.19, probably also with reference to Col. 2.9.

Refut. V.12.5	Refut. VIII.13.2	Col. 1.19	Col. 2.9
	ὅτι	ὅτι ἐν αὐτῷ εὐδόκησεν	ὅτι ἐν αὐτῷ
πᾶν	πᾶν	πᾶν	
τὸ πλήρωμα	τὸ πλήρωμα	τὸ πλήρωμα	
εὐδόκησε	ηὐδόκησε		
κατοικῆσαι	κατοικῆσαι	κατοικῆσαι	κατοικεῖ πᾶν τὸ πλήρωμα τῆς θεότητος
ἐν	ἐπὶ τὸν υἱὸν		
αὐτῷ	τοῦ ἀνθρώπου		
σωματικῶς	σωματικῶς		σωματικῶς
καὶ πᾶσά			
ἐστιν ἐν αὐτῷ			
ἡ θεότης			

There are several factors here, however, which deserve our notice. In word order there stands a similarity shared by the Peratae and Monoïmus,[30] and they combine key words which are found in distinct though related sayings in Colossians. This could

27 So in *Refut.* V. 16.12 John 1.1–4 is quoted.
28 Hippolytus, *Refut.* V.12.5.
29 Hippolytus, *Refut.* VIII.13.2.
30 The followers of Colorbasus were said to have called the saviour *Eudocetus* 'because the whole pleroma was pleased (ὅτι πᾶν τὸ πλήρωμα ηὐδόκησεν) through him to glorify the Father' (Irenaeus, *Adv. Haer.* I.12.4). We are clearly dealing with the same tradition and this use helps to show its popularity, but the reference is too brief to be of much assistance to us here.

be explained as the result of a form of tradition which grew up in dependence upon Colossians, but it might also suggest that there may have been a yet earlier formula which has guided the formation of all these sayings. Our credence in this possibility may be furthered by the fact that the author of Colossians seems to refer twice to the general formula, perhaps indicating that he was making use of older tradition.[31] It may also be that the Peratae had knowledge of a kind of expansion of the formula[32] which would help to explain the language of Col. 2.9. This could, then, tell us why Colossians uses separately the distinctive words εὐδόκησε and σωματικῶς which are combined twice elsewhere.

If we are willing on this basis to look for a source of tradition prior to the writing of Colossians, we may next notice that the contexts for three of the versions set out above have to do with the begetting or 'birth' of the saviour. In the fourth context (Col. 2.9 with 2.11f.) the author goes on to write of the new birth by baptism of the Colossian Christians. With these clues in hand we are suddenly and strikingly reminded of the story of Jesus' baptism or birth as the 'Son' as it is best attested in the text of Luke 3.22: καὶ καταβῆναι τὸ πνεῦμα τὸ ἅγιον σωματικῷ εἴδει ὡς περιστερὰν ἐπ' αὐτόν, καὶ φωνὴν ἐξ οὐρανοῦ γενέσθαι, σὺ εἶ ὁ υἱός μου ὁ ἀγαπητός, ἐν σοὶ εὐδόκησα.

Commentators tend to suggest that it is Luke himself who has supplied the rather dramatic σωματικῷ,[33] though we are now in a position to ask if its use in a presumably pre-Lucan (or at least contemporary) Colossians does not suggest pre-Lucan tradition for this understanding. What is more, we may now have a better insight into the reason for the use of σωματικῶς in Col. 2.9 as well as by the Peratae and Monoïmus, a conception which has puzzled many commentators.[34] The author of the epistle would, in these terms, have been influenced by an older form of tradition, perhaps one which pictured the *divinity* represented by the dove or in some

[31] Referring to Col. 1.19 and 2.9, O. Michel maintains that 'this obviously belongs to the fixed liturgical and kerygmatical stock of the community' (*TWNT* V, 154).

[32] In *Refut.* X.10.4, where the views of the Peratae are summarized, the version given is ἐν ᾧ κατοικεῖ πᾶν τὸ πλήρωμα τῆς θεότητος σωματι(κῶς). This much closer correspondence to Col. 2.9 may, however, here be the result of Hippolytus' knowledge of that text.

[33] Cf. Creed, *The Gospel according to St Luke*, 57.

[34] Cf. C. F. D. Moule, *The Epistles of Paul the Apostle to the Colossians and to Philemon* (Cambridge Greek Testament Commentary), Cambridge 1957, 92ff.

other fashion, coming down upon Jesus. Emphasis was then placed upon the reality or materiality of this visitation.[35] At another stage, perhaps now under the influence of a more obviously proto-gnostic movement or in opposition to it, stress came to be laid upon the *fullness* of the presence of the divinity.

Something of a similar nature might be said about the reference to the *dwelling* of the divinity, although here we have a suspicion that we may, in fact, be dealing with a much older understanding regarding the presence of the divinity whether conceived of symbolically or in actuality. Κατοικέω is regularly used in the LXX to translate both YŠB and ŠKN, words which themselves are often employed to indicate the dwelling or tabernacling of the deity. The word, therefore, has strong cultic[36] and liturgical associations and may belong to an older context of ideas involving the narratives of the baptism and transfiguration (the latter with its σκηναί, divine presence and voice).[37] In this connection we may note that Monoïmus could preserve the more primitive and Semitic understanding when he speaks of the fullness dwelling ἐπί rather than ἐν. So Luke's version of the baptismal narrative also tells of the Spirit in bodily form coming down ἐπ' αὐτόν.[38]

We may next suggest that this hypothesis could offer some assistance in understanding the use of εὐδόκησε(ν) (or ηὐδόκησε) in Col. 1.19 and the two sayings recorded by Hippolytus. It is aorist and 'adoptionistic' because it is dependent on that which was originally conceived of as a liturgical-*cum*-mythical event in time

[35] Although C. H. Talbert also contends that Luke himself supplied this understanding and suggests the intention 'to prevent any separation between Spirit and flesh in Jesus', such a purpose may come across far more clearly in the tradition as it is expressed in Colossians. In this fashion our hypothesis might be used to give some general support to Talbert's thesis regarding the anti-gnostic or at least anti-docetic tendencies in Luke, though in this instance Luke was in touch with and made use of a tradition already developing in this direction and did not fashion it himself. See Talbert's *Luke and the Gnostics*, Nashville/New York 1966, 112, and 'An Anti-Gnostic Tendency in Lucan Christology', *NTS* 14, 1967/8, 267.

[36] Cf. Michel, *TWNT* V, 153. For the combination of God's pleasure in having a temple in which to dwell among men, see II Macc. 14.35.

[37] Cf. *SMMH*, 365ff., 382ff., where we understand these two scenes to be variant presentations of sacral ordination.

[38] As does Matt. 3.15. Mark 1.10 probably read εἰς αὐτόν, although a number of texts have ἐπ'. There may well be a 'Q' understanding here which is prior to Mark's, though both may be regarded as translation variants representing slightly different nuances. Both, however, differ significantly from the more metaphysical idea of union represented by ἐν αὐτῷ.

which came also to be interpreted in historical terms.[39] The subject of the verb may now appear somewhat uncertain,[40] again because the earlier framework was not that of metaphysical thought. At one time the subject was a voice 'from heaven' conceived of either independently or perhaps as speaking through the symbol of the divine presence.

We are now willing to ask if there may not be another aspect (along with his use of ἐπί) of Monoïmus's version which could reach back to an earlier stage in the history of this tradition. It will obviously be regarded as highly speculative when we suggest that this later teacher could also have better preserved an understanding of the object of this divine visitation. Others would doubtless be content to regard his use of the Son of Man in this connection as due to his concern with the figure otherwise. One must, however, also recognize that he could have introduced the statement into this context because it was already connected with the designation.[41] We have, in addition, found reason, with others before us, to ask whether logia such as John 1.51 (the angels of God[42] ascending and descending ἐπὶ τὸν υἱὸν τοῦ ἀνθρώπου) and John 6.27 might not suggest a time at which Jesus' baptism was understood as the ordination of one who was to act as the Son of Man.[43] Along with this we must take into account several other traditions which we have discussed or will discuss which closely link the Son of Man designation with baptism[44] and even more frequently with some conception of anthropogenesis. It is in these terms that we would suggest the possibility that Monoïmus's form of this tradition might not be regarded as entirely his own creation and unique,

[39] There may be a dependence upon Isa. 42.1 or 62.4, though in neither case is such a derivation obvious. L. B. Radford suggests that it may be a kind of timeless aorist, but admits, 'At first sight the past tense of the verb seems to suggest that the Son's deity was conferred at some point in time' (*The Epistle to the Colossians and the Epistle to Philemon* [Westminster Commentaries], London 1931, 182).

[40] See Moule, *op. cit.*, 70f.

[41] It may be worth noticing that the short version of the formula under discussion found in Irenaeus, *Adv. Haer.* I.12.4, is bound in close context with two references to the Son of Man. See above, p. 66 n. 30, and pp. 59f.

[42] This may be regarded as another way of referring to the divine presence and favour and one perhaps even more readily capable of being transformed into the idea of 'all the fullness'.

[43] Cf. *SMMH*, 278ff., 295ff., and again at 365ff.

[44] See especially p. 60 above, and below on several passages in the Gospel of Philip.

but rather as dependent upon some earlier stage of belief and practice.

This Monoïmus, styled 'the Arabian' by Hippolytus, was among those who spoke of the high God as the Anthropos. He constitutes a single monad which comprises all opposites.[45] He is the perfect and invisible Man[46] who can be called τὸ πᾶν.[47] Monoïmus also maintained

that this Son of (the) Man (υἱὸν ἀνθρώπου) already mentioned is begotten and subject to passion. He is generated independently of time, undesignedly[48] and without being predestinated. For such, he says, is the power of that Man. His power being such, the Son was born more quickly than thought and volition. And so it is, he maintains, written in the scriptures, 'He was and was generated' (ἦν καὶ ἐγένετο); this means, Man was and his Son was generated.[49]

Monoïmus' reference in this last sentence is not wholly clear. While there might be a play on John 1.1-3, this is far from certain. The understanding of the Son of Man as subject to passion (παθητόν) may suggest the Christ of Christian faith, though, it must be recognized, some such an idea is almost a commonplace in myths about the creation of the first earthly man when he is compared to his heavenly archetype.[50] Since the myth of creation is the context for this reference to the Son of Man, it may be more consistent to interpret παθητόν in that setting than in some other, and this may be for us a valuable hint pointing to one of the early contexts for such language.

Other passages drawn from Monoïmus and dealing with the Son of Man are more obscure and esoteric.

[45] *Refut.* VIII.12.5.

[46] *Refut.* VIII.12.7.

[47] *Refut.* VIII.12.2.

[48] Ἀβουλήτως is apparently intended as an emphasis on the absolutely free manner in which the Son was generated. It is, however, an emendation for ἀβασιλεύτως which could mean 'without royalty'. This would make sense in that the Son of Man does not rule like the Man, is subject to passion, etc. Yet it seems rather out of context in this sequence. There is a reference to the ἀβασίλευτος generation from the blessed Man in the Naassene mythology (*Refut.* V.8.2) which might suggest that such was intended here also, or one might believe that it helped to cause the alteration here.

[49] *Refut.* VIII.12.2-4.

[50] Thus the non-Christian Poimandres (*Corpus Hermeticum.* I.15) speaks of the *man* on earth as being dual in nature and says that he τὰ θνητὰ πάσχει ὑποκείμενος τῇ εἱμαρμένῃ. 'Though he is superior to the framework, he has become a slave (δοῦλος) in it.'

The Son of Man (ὁ υἱὸς τοῦ ἀνθρώπου), therefore, he says to have been generated from the perfect Man whom no one knew. Every creature who is ignorant of the Son, however, forms an idea as a female off-spring. Certain very obscure rays of this Son which approach this world check and control and change generation. And the beauty of that Son of Man (ἐκείνου τοῦ υἱοῦ τοῦ ἀνθρώπου) is up to the present in-comprehensible to all men, as many as are led astray concerning the offspring of the female.[51]

Once more the context is that of the creation or generation of the *son* of the God-Man. Again the myth conceives of the Man as invisible and unknown, while the *son* is at least to some degree knowable as his manifestation. This much relates the passage to those studied above which were drawn from the followers of Colorbasus and Marcus and from the Ophites. Monoïmus, then, goes on to give this Son of the Man a definite role in the mainte-nance of the creation.

Monoïmus also seems to be conducting a kind of polemic, though the precise target is not easy to determine. Is he suggesting that Jesus could not have been the Son of Man because he was born of a woman? Such might help us to understand why there is little in Hippolytus' report which would indicate that Monoïmus espoused a specifically Christian faith. Or is it, as for instance in passages to be discussed below from the pseudo-Clementine literature,[52] John the Baptist who is alluded to as 'the offspring of the female'. Yet, although either of these concerns may have influenced Monoïmus, we are more probably dealing with an attitude which became typical for a number of gnostics who main-tained that all derived from or related to the female principle in the world was inferior to the male. This understanding itself can, however, be regarded as a development from certain tendencies already present in late Judaism.[53]

The high God, as generally among the gnostics, is not regarded by Monoïmus as the creator. Unlike many of the gnostic systems, however, the very first principle generated by the God-Man is said to have acted creatively. One suspects that this is indicative of a less-developed form of gnostic speculation which has not yet determined that the entire creation is evil. Correspondingly there

[51] Hippolytus, *Refut.* VIII.13.3–4.
[52] See below, pp. 75ff. There, however, the language of Matt. 11.11 is definitely used, while here this is not manifest.
[53] E.g. I Enoch 54.8; Test. Reuben 5.3.

has not yet evolved the more complex system of emanations from the One above who would then bear no responsibility for the created world.

All things, however, have been produced not from entirety (ἀπὸ ὅλου), but from some part of the Son of Man (τοῦ υἱοῦ τοῦ ἀνθρώπου). For, he says, the Son of Man is a jot, one tittle proceeding from above, full and replenishing all. This has in itself whatever things the Man also has, the Father of the Son of Man.[54]

This last image, here rather obscurely expressed, is made somewhat more clear in the previous passage. The Son of Man is compared to the superscripted mark which when placed above the iota indicates the number ten. Thus does the Son of Man, as one uncompounded and simple tittle, yet compound and make multiform. So is he also 'an image of that perfect invisible Man'.[55]

A somewhat similar understanding may be reflected elsewhere in Hippolytus' survey when we are informed, by means of teachings said to have been garnered from the Naassenes, that there stand in the temple of the Samothracians two images of naked men. They are said to be images respectively of the primal Man (ἀρχάνθρωπος), whom they call Adam, and the spiritual one born again in every respect of the same substance with that man (κατὰ πάνθ' ὁμοουσίου ἐκείνω τῷ ἀνθρώπῳ).[56] In this case, however, the second man referred to is apparently the gnostic believer, while the Archanthropos is probably to be regarded as the saviour, the Son of the high God, and not the high God himself. Indeed, the explanation of the *substantial* unity of the Primal Man and the believer is given in terms of a reference to a tradition closely related to several logia found in the canonical Gospels. It is, however, interesting that in a saying so clearly reminiscent of John 6.53 a mention of the Son of Man is absent.[57]

ἐὰν μὴ πίνητέ μου τὸ αἷμα καὶ φάγητέ μου τὴν σάρκα, οὐ μὴ εἰσέλθητε εἰς τὴν βασιλείαν τῶν οὐρανῶν. ἀλλὰ κἂν πίητε, φησί, τὸ ποτήριον ὃ ἐγὼ πίνω, ὅπου ἐγὼ ὑπάγω, ἐκεῖ ὑμεῖς εἰσελθεῖν οὐ δύνασθε.[58]

[54] Hippolytus, *Refut.* VIII.13.4.
[55] Hippolytus, *Refut.* VIII.12.7.
[56] *Refut.* V.8.9–10.
[57] Similar is the Gospel of Philip, saying 23. Cf. below, p. 82.
[58] *Refut.* V.8.11. The Naassenes have apparently purposefully distorted the sense of the traditions in order to suggest that not all of the disciples were to be saved.

This passage also illustrates the heavy dependence of the Naassenes upon Christian lore, though some scholars have long contended that these Christian features are accretions to the earlier beliefs of these sectarians.[59]

Yet stronger parallels with the teaching of Monoïmus seem to have been espoused by the Naassenes, the parallels being so obvious that the two systems must, at the least, be closely related.[60] At this juncture of thought, however, the Man and the Son of Man are fully identified. The Naassenes honoured as the originator of all things one who could be entitled both Man and Son of Man (ἄνθρωπον καὶ υἰὸν ἀνθρώπου).[61] This Man is regarded as a hermaphrodite[62] who can be called Adamas.[63]

'It is from this blessed Man above or Archanthropos or Adamantos, as it seems to them, that souls have been conveyed down here into a creation of clay.'[64] It is fundamental to the Naassene belief that men below are, as it were, copies of the perfect Man above. Here they must suffer and seek to ascend whence they have come. The basic myth, therefore, is concerned with the image of the perfect Adam above. This image can itself also be styled 'the perfect Man'.[65] He is the portrayed one from the unportrayable, the inner Man who has fallen from the Archanthropos.[66] This Adam below must suffer in 'many waters' and be regarded 'as a worm and no man' before arising to be 'the King of glory'.[67] The manner in which all true gnostics are involved in

---

The relationship with Johannine tradition is demonstrated by the use of *flesh* and blood rather than the synoptic body and blood and by the general structure (though eating flesh comes first in John) and wording of the opening protasis. The gnostic tradition then, however, appears to have reference to a tradition like Mark 10.38 (= Matt. 20.22) and closes with words strongly reminiscent of John 8.21 and 13.33.

[59] Cf. *SMMH*, 56 n. 2.
[60] See R. P. Casey, 'Naassenes and Ophites', *JTS* 27, 1926, 374ff.
[61] *Refut.* V.6.4. This originating principle may also be referred to as the Logos, but the text is difficult at this point and no attempt at emendation is entirely satisfactory. On the Man and Son of Man seemingly viewed as one, see further below, p. 107 n. 185.
[62] On this characteristic see above, pp. 62f.
[63] *Refut.* V.6.5; see V.8.2.
[64] *Refut.* V.7.30.
[65] See *Refut.* V.8.21.
[66] *Refut.* V.7.36.
[67] See *Refut.* V.8.15–19.

this myth is made clear when it is maintained that the Christ 'in all that have been generated is the portrayed Son of Man (υἱὸς ἀνθρώπου) from the unportrayable Logos'.[68]

We notice that while earlier the Son of Man was employed as an alternative designation for the originating principle, here a distinction of sorts seems to be drawn. The Son of Man, then, exists as though God above, but also is portrayed in those on earth. Are two different mythical conceptions here combined, or, as in the canonical Gospels, is there a sense in which the Son of Man exists in two phases, as a divine being and in human form on earth? In our earlier study we suggested that, however much the Naassenes had borrowed from established Christian materials, it is at least possible to discern in their lore an earlier set of understandings regarding a man-like hero, reminiscent of beliefs and practices from yet older mythologies, who must suffer (through water) before arising to glory. Either this was derived from primitive Christian understandings or it first existed (as we think) as a sectarian Jewish parallel to ideas which affected Christian beginnings.[69] In any event, we once more notice that the Son of Man designation is several times employed without direct reference to any of the logia or even to any of the language associated with the title in canonical materials.

Finally, in connection with reports by Irenaeus and Hippolytus regarding gnostic employment of the Son of Man designation, we find a single reference in the system of Justin the Gnostic. Baruch, the heavenly messenger, speaks to Jesus.

All the prophets before you have been enticed. Put forth an effort, therefore, Jesus, Son of Man (υἱὲ ἀνθρώπου), not to be allured, but to preach this word to men and make known to them the things concerning the Father and things concerning the Good One.[70]

This usage is strikingly singular in all the Son of Man materials studied in that the designation is found in the vocative. Jesus himself is directly addressed as Son of Man. One surmises, however, that even with Justin such was not typical, since it is the only reference to the Son of Man to be found in material attributed to him.

[68] *Refut.* V.7.33.
[69] See *SMMH*, especially 181ff.
[70] *Refut.* V.26.30.

Actually Jesus himself hardly plays a dominant role in Justin's system, and he appears only before his ascension, i.e. as an earthly figure. This, together with the context and the following mention of the ἄνθρωποι to whom the message is to be preached, could well suggest that the writer has taken the designation to be a reference to the human status of Jesus. If this be so, one may believe that the author's affinities, in so far as the use of this title is concerned, are with that form of understanding found in Ignatius, Barnabas and Irenaeus' own theology.[71] It is there seen as a way of indicating Jesus' humanity and, as such, is directly connected neither with the usage in the canonical Gospels nor with the usage found elsewhere among gnostics.

2. REFERENCES IN GNOSTIC WRITINGS

We shall now deal with references to the Son of Man drawn directly from gnostic writings, and we come first to three passages from the pseudo-Clementine literature. We include them here because they each exhibit the influence of gnostic themes. If this represents a relatively late influence,[72] then these references to the Son of Man could also belong to the third century and be of relatively little significance for our study. It may be, however, that earlier Son of Man references have later been interpreted in a gnostic manner. Alternatively, portions of the earliest strata of material for this literature, including these passages, could have been formulated by an earlier Jewish-Christian group already undergoing gnosticizing influences.[73] We incline toward this latter understanding.

For our purposes it is significant that the pseudo-Clementine works are usually traced to Syria or an immediately adjacent area and also that traditions associated with prominent sectarian figures like Simon Magus and John Baptist play important roles. The connection with aspects of the sectarian movements of this general area is further suggested by the reported strict vegetarianism of Peter and by the use only of water in the Eucharist. As in

[71] See above, pp. 37ff., and especially p. 38 n. 24 on comparable references in 'On the Resurrection' and in a version of the closing verses of the *Didache*. Compare the form of address in Ezek. 2.1, etc.

[72] Cf. J. Irmscher, *NTA* II, 532ff.

[73] See G. Strecker, *Das Judenchristentum in den Pseudoklementinen* (TU 70), 1958.

several other gnostic and/or Jewish(-Christian) sectarian writings, a concern with the chrism as a 'sacrament' appears to have supplanted baptism or to have surpassed it in importance. Like many another gnostic and/or sectarian writing, these pseudo-Clementine works also evidence an interest in anthropogony and in Adam as the first man.

In *Homilies* III.22 Peter, having told of Adam, the first anointed and only true prophet,[74] in that the Spirit of Christ (later manifested in other forms and names, finally known in the anointed Jesus)[75] was his, tells of the creation of the female companion, one very different from Adam. She is obviously inferior and represents the *paired*[76] female principle now ruling in the world. She is also the first prophetess, and from her springs an inferior line of prophecy, 'all those born of women. But the other (i.e. Adam), as son of Man (ὡς υἱὸς ἀνθρώπου), being a male, prophesies better things to the world to come as a male.'[77]

This passage must be compared with *Recognitions* I.60, where the matter under discussion and the principle of interpretation are similar. One of John Baptist's disciples contends that John, not Jesus, was the Christ, since Jesus himself maintained that John was greater than all men and all prophets. To this Simon, the Canaanite,[78] replies that 'John was indeed greater than all the prophets and all who are born of women (*filii mulierum*), yet that he is not greater than a Son of Man (*filio hominis*)'.[79]

The argument in the two passages is based upon a clear and well-established gnostic theme: the priority and superiority of the spiritual male principle to that of the hylic female. We may compare the Gospel of Thomas, logion 15: 'When you see him who was not born of woman, prostrate yourselves upon your face and adore him; he is your Father.'[80] Just as obviously the tradition

[74] Cf. Strecker, *op. cit.*, 145ff.

[75] *Hom.* III.20 and 21.

[76] *Hom.* III.23.1: the female (i.e. with reference to John the Baptist) 'has been appointed to come first in the advent of pairs' (ἐν τῇ τῶν συζυγιῶν). See below on the pairs or syzygies.

[77] *Hom.* III.22.3. To this degree, Colpe may not be quite correct when he maintains (*TWNT* VIII, 478) that the designation refers *only* to Jesus in the pseudo-Clementine material.

[78] In the tradition of gnostic works certain disciples are given an opportunity to speak or respond in turn.

[79] *Rec.* I.60.3.

[80] Compare also Thomas, log. 106: 'When you make the two one, you

found in Matt. 11.9 ('. . . Yes, I tell you, and more than a prophet') is basic to the thought along with Matt. 11.11a: 'Truly, I say to you, among those born of women there has arisen no one greater than John the Baptist.'[81] Furthermore, it is evident that, although the formulators of these materials (or at least the formulators of the traditions which they were using) appear to have been aware of the titular connotations of the Son of Man designation (see below on *Recognitions* III.61.2), they have made use of the designation for their own purposes.

We must, therefore, here regard the references to the Son of Man as secondary to the traditions found in the canonical Gospels and as occasioned by certain forms of Christian understanding. On the other hand, we cannot overlook the wider context of motifs here associated with the use of the expression. The designation may only have been employed in these contexts because of a certain esoteric appeal and/or due to its usefulness for the manner of argumentation here made. It is possible, however, though not demonstrable, that the designation was used because it still had some currency among Jewish-gnostic-Christian sectarians. It could point back to a line of tradition in which the term once had a greater popularity.[82]

This last possibility may be somewhat enhanced by the third reference to the Son of Man in this literature. In *Recognitions* III.61 the author is speaking of the ten pairs (*paria*) which have been assigned to this world from the beginning of time. He begins with Cain and Abel and passes on through various Old Testament figures until (III.61.2) he comes to the seventh, the tempter and the Son of Man (*filii hominis*). We are hardly surprised to find in such a gnosticizing content a reference to the syzygies; nor is it very surprising that the Son of Man should come to be regarded as one of them. (The heavenly Anthropos, as we have seen, is a member of a syzygy in several of the Valentinian-like accounts.)

---

shall become sons of the Man' (*nshēre mprōme*), i.e. 'Man' here used especially in the sense of the male principle.

[81] Compare the use of Matt. 11.11 in Thomas, log. 46. It is, of course, possible that the pseudo-Clementines are not dependent upon canonical Matthew for this tradition, but this issue is of no consequence for our present purposes.

[82] Cf. above, p. 49 n. 48.

What is rather unusual is the presentation of earthly syzygies of whom the Son of Man is one.[83]

We shall next concern ourselves with the Coptic gnostic documents which preserve references to the Son of Man designation in the context of writings evidently passed on through long years of gnostic belief and practice. We first examine three passages from the Gospel of Philip.

> The Lord went into the dye-works
> of Levi. He took seventy-two colours
> and threw them into the vat. He took them
> all out white. And he said: 'Even so
> came the Son of
> (the Son of) Man . . .'
>
> (Gospel of Philip, saying 54; 111.25–30)

The text in lines 29f. reads *shēre mpshēre mprōm*[*e*], and the translators suggest dittography. The issue is complicated, however, by the expression 'the seed of the Son of Man' in saying 102 and especially by 'the son of the Son of Man' (*pshēre mpshēre mprōme*) found twice in saying 120 and in a version of the Epistle of Eugnostos,[84] as well as the idea that Seth was made in the image of the Son of Man found in versions of the Apocryphon of John.[85] Although the *pshēre* in line 30 of the saying above is marked for cancelling, it would seem that the intention of the author of Philip must be decided on exegetical rather than textual grounds.

In Philip, saying 43, God is said to be a dyer who can make men immortal with immortal dyes.[86] 'God dips (*baptizes*) what he dips (*baptizes*) in water.'[87] It would appear that *dyeing* is a way of talking about baptism, and this would suggest that saying 54 could be read with the same frame of reference in mind.[88] In these terms we

[83] Also unusual, in comparison with other gnostic schemes, is the fact that the pairs are seen wholly as opposites.

[84] See below, p. 96. Cf. also above on the conception of the Man and Son of Man having a 'son', which Irenaeus has preserved.

[85] See below, pp. 109f.

[86] Some would here refer us to the story of the magic feat of dyeing by the boy Jesus in the Infancy Gospel of Thomas (cf. *NTA* I, 400f.), but aspects of a common derivation are at least not evident.

[87] Cf. E. Segelberg, 'The Coptic-Gnostic Gospel according to Philip and its Sacramental System', *Numen* 7, 1960, 192.

[88] See R. McL. Wilson, *The Gospel of Philip*, London 1962, 114f. Here and in the following we are drawing largely from Wilson's translation.

might find here a reference to the coming of the Son of Man into the world through his baptism, and the text, then, originally intended a reference to the Son of Man and not any 'son of . . .'[89]

We must also recognize, however, that 'Lord' (*c̆oeis*) regularly refers to Jesus in this Gospel, and there is no instance of it being used unambiguously for God.[90] In light of this factor Jesus-Lord and Son of Man may be seen as the dyer and not the one dyed. The seventy-two colours might be regarded as symbolic of all nations, i.e. all disciples.[91] The references in lines 29f. may then be to the son(s), the believers, of the Son of Man who are *born* in this manner.

While gnostic writings are crowded with what appears to be obscure symbolism, and one cannot regularly make an argument from such, the opacity of the details here together with both the parallels and divergencies in saying 43 might well suggest a larger background of thought which has then been made severely elliptical. We would accordingly suspect that saying 54 could reach back to understandings older than the Gospel of Philip itself.

> A horse begets a horse,
> a man begets man, a god
> begets god. So it is with the bride-
> groom and the bride. [Their children]
> originate from the bridal chamber.
> There was no Jew [who came]
> from the Greeks [so long as the law]
> existed, and [we too had our]
> [origin] from the Jews [before we became]
> Christians . . . .

[89] W. C. Till (*Das Evangelium nach Philippos*, Berlin 1963) proposes 'as a dyer' to complete line 30. Similar is J. É. Ménard, *L'Évangile selon Philippe*, Paris 1964, 1967. H.-M. Schenke (with J. Leipoldt, *Koptisch-gnostische Schriften aus den Papyrus-Codices von Nag-Hamadi* (Theologische Forschung 20), Hamburg-Bergstedt 1960, suggests 'in order to take away defects', [um] die Fehler [wegzunehmen], but, as Wilson points out, any restoration here must remain highly conjectural.

[90] Cf. 103.34, 37; 104.16; 107.7, 24; 110.6; 112.10; 115.27; 116.6, 27; 122.12, 25; 126.22, 25; 129.16.

[91] The figure would be derived either from Luke 10.1, 17 or from a similar background of thought from which Luke borrowed the idea. None of these references are, however, easy to pin down. Since this is the only reference to Levi in Philip, an attempt to connect it with some other Levitical theme or writing would be but guesswork.

> and they called them . . . .
> the chosen race of the . . . . . .
> and the true Man and the Son
> of Man and the seed of the Son of Man.
> This race they call true
> in the world.
>
> (Gospel of Philip, saying 102; 123.25–124.4)

This passage is marred by many problems with the text. Almost every line on page 123 involves some form of conjecture. The last line (36) reads *pgenos etsotp mp* [. . . = the chosen race of the [. . . Restorations such as *mp[noute]* = of God, or *mp[iot]* = of the Father, or *mp[pnā etouaab]* = of the Holy Spirit, are suggested. The problem runs over into the next lines (124.1–2), where the references to the true Man and the Son of Man (*auō palētheinos rrōme auō pshēre/mprōme*) could be taken (so Schenke) as continuing the genitive, i.e. 'the chosen race of the [. . . . . .] and of the Man and of the Son of Man'.[92] In this case, 'the seed (σπέρμα) of the Son of Man' would probably be a second name for the group. It is as likely, however, that 'true Man' and 'Son of Man' are here intended as other *names* for the chosen race and that the titles stand in apposition. This would certainly be in keeping with teaching such as that found among the Naassenes as set out above. The race is called by the name, as it were, of its divine *eponym*.

There are a number of other references to 'the Man'[93] in this Gospel and in most cases it is either explicitly or implicitly clear that Jesus is meant. This usage might be viewed as a form of christological development in that Jesus is given a title attributed in other gnostic writings to the high God. We notice, however, as in certain other gnostic materials, that the two titles Man and Son of Man are directly linked. Since it would seem that Jesus is the Son of Man in sayings 54 and 120 (see below), one can only assume that both titles were here meant to refer to Jesus, although there may have been an earlier stage when the applications were differentiated, giving a sequence of Man = high God or his emanation; Son of Man = the emanation or image of the Man (sometimes regarded as the saviour) and son of the Son of Man = the first

---

[92] Cf. 106.20 and the reference there to 'the sons of the perfect man'.
[93] Perfect Man = 103.12; 106.20; 108.23f.; 123.19, 21; 124.22f.; 128.4; Man of Heaven = 106.17; Living Man = 123.22. Cf. also 106.31.

true gnostic (regarded either as the true believer or himself as the saviour).[94]

The major themes of saying 102 are consonant with interests evident throughout this Gospel. Motifs having to do with creation and begetting are prominent, as is a concern with such well-established sectarian motifs as the bridegroom, the bride, spiritual marriage and the bridechamber. It is evident that in several gnostic groups, among them such widely separated sects as the Marcosians[95] and the Mandaeans,[96] these motifs played an important role in the initiatory service. This association is also abundantly clear in such sayings as 31, 66, 67, 68, 76, 95, 125 and 127 from this Gospel of Philip, where baptism, chrism, the bridechamber and endowment with light are closely related. As with saying 54, then, the Son of Man is found in context with motifs related to baptism.

Saying 120 is not directly concerned with baptism, but it does concentrate on the themes of creation and begetting.

> There is the Son of Man
> and there is the son of the Son of
> Man. The Lord is the Son of
> Man and the son of the Son of
> Man is he who is created[97] through the
> Son of Man. The Son of Man received
> from God the power to create. He
> has (also) the ability to beget.
>
> (Gospel of Philip, saying 120; 129.14–21)

[94] Again on this tripartite conception see below, pp. 95ff. Wilson (*op. cit.,* 163) mentions the possibility that this idea of the race of the Son of Man is derived from Dan. 7.27 (where the kingdom and the dominion are given to the saints of the Most High) in conjunction with Dan. 7.13. This derivation is conceivable whether the 'saints' were originally intended as divine beings or men (on the passage cf. *SMMH*, 144), but there are few signs of a gnostic and/or Christian form of tradition which would support this derivation.

[95] Cf. Irenaeus, *Adv. Haer.* I.13.6; 21.3ff. On the relationship of the practices of these groups, cf. E. Segelberg, *Maṣbūtā. Studies in the Ritual of Mandaean Baptism*, Uppsala 1958, 167ff. Note that some of the esoteric words of the Marcosians, listed by Irenaeus in *Adv. Haer.* I.21.3, can probably best be explained in close relationship with Mandaean terminology. Compare especially the Marcosian κουστά and the Mandaean *kušṭa*, the ritual handclasp ceremony often used in association with the baptismal rite.

[96] Cf. Segelberg, *op. cit., passim.*

[97] Schenke, C. J. de Catanzaro ('The Gospel of Philip', *JTS* ns 13, 1962, 35–71) and Wilson take *petsōnt* as intransitive and passive, while Till sees it as active ('he who creates through the Son of Man'). Even though the latter use of the verb predominates (cf. Wilson, *op. cit.,* 180, and see in the next

We notice again that the title Lord, elsewhere indicative of Jesus, is given to the Son of Man. We see also that the Son of Man is, in this case, clearly differentiated from God.[98] He is apparently conceived of as a cosmic figure who has been endowed with God's own creative power. (We may think of John 1.1ff.; Col. 1.15ff. and Heb. 1.2 where, on the basis of different christological ideas drawn from older Jewish materials, the same power is attributed to Christ as of the Word, Image and Son respectively.) The reference to his ability to beget apparently distinguishes the capacity to form his *children*, and 'the son of the Son of Man'[99] is probably here regarded as the gnostic believer formed in some likeness to the Son of Man.[100] In one sense the whole of the Gospel of Philip might be seen as devoted to understanding the proper begetting of this 'son'.

We notice that, although Philip's author(s) knew either one or more of the canonical Gospels or material which was also incorporated into these Gospels, there is not a hint of a direct influence by any of the Son of Man logia now found in the New Testament. We do, however, find at 105.4–5: 'He who will not eat my flesh (σάρξ) and drink my blood has no life in him.' This, of course, demands a comparison with John 6.53: 'Unless you eat the flesh (σάρξ) and drink the blood of the Son of Man you have no life in you.' The distinctive use of σάρξ (as opposed to σῶμα as in the synoptic and Pauline accounts of the Last Supper) appears to make the relationship clear. Either John has added a reference

---

Philip saying 121; 129.23, 25, 28 [32], though with attendant problems), the passive seems to make the preferable sense. Again, however, the matter is complicated by the following saying, which seems carefully to distinguish the power of creation from that of begetting, the latter being done in secret also being the greater. But it is at least not clear that this distinction is preserved in saying 120.

[98] It is interesting to find that God (*noute*) is on a number of occasions used for the good, high God in Philip. In many other gnostic writings the word is avoided or it becomes a designation for an inferior being. (Cf. e.g. Thomas, log. 100.) This could indicate that Philip is an 'early' gnostic work, though such deductions are hazardous, and it may only indicate that Philip stood closer to more orthodox Christian thought.

[99] Philip, saying 74, speaks of being born through the Holy Spirit and born again through Christ.

[100] A version of the Epistle of Eugnostos, however, viewed the son of the Son of Man as a saviour figure. See below, pp. 96ff. On the interpretation in Philip, cf. Ménard, *op. cit.*, 237.

to the Son of Man or Philip or his tradition has dropped it. In the latter event it becomes even less apparent that Philip's author had a proclivity for usage of the Son of Man designation, and, in either case, the absence of the designation here points up this seeming lack of relationship between most gnostic uses of the title and those found in the New Testament.[101]

It is, of course, still far from impossible that all of the language in the Gospel of Philip referring to the Son of Man who has the power to create and beget and to the son of the Son of Man and the seed of the Son of Man was originally fashioned to serve Christian gnostic purposes. As we proceed, however, we shall wish to propose another context which may well have been prior – a context in which it was the great hero made in the image of Man (often Adam) and his son (often Seth, from whom many further gnostic 'sons' traced their descent) who were known by these designations.[102]

We have previously seen that the Gospel of Thomas (or its earlier tradition) may also have omitted the Son of Man title in materials like logia 21b, 103[103] and quite possibly 44 as well.[104] Otherwise there are no uses of the designation in Thomas, except in logion 86, which stands as an obvious parallel to the Q saying of Matt. 8.20 = Luke 9.58.

> Jesus said: [The foxes]
> [have] the[ir] holes and the birds have
> [their] nest, but the Son of Man
> has no place to lay his head and
> to rest.

The last two words represent a typical gnostic addition and interpretation.[105]

While this gnostic-type collection of sayings seems to stand closer than any other gnostic work to the traditions found in the synoptic Gospels, it discloses only this degree of relationship with the canonical uses of the Son of Man title. We have seen that some might suggest this to be due to Thomas's derivation from very early materials, perhaps before the Son of Man designation became

[101] On a similar use of John 6.53 among the Naassenes, see above, p. 72.
[102] See below, especially pp. 109f.
[103] See above, pp. 13ff.
[104] See above, p. 9, n. 35.
[105] Cf. Gärtner, *Theology of Thomas*, 61; R. Kasser, *L'Évangile selon Thomas*, Neuchâtel 1961, 104; M. L. Peel, *The Epistle to Rheginos*, London 1969, 142.

firmly rooted and grew in the Christian traditions. We have given our reasons for believing that such a contention involves an erroneous understanding both of the values of Thomas and of the origin of the Son of Man in the traditions behind the Gospels. The theory that Thomas reflects the status of the title in very early Christian materials might also tend, at the least, to complicate the views of those scholars who find the beginnings of the usage of the Son of Man in eschatological statements and who regard the references to the earthly Son of Man as secondary.[106] Rather do we contend that in this manner, as in others, Thomas is witness to typical later gnostic understandings which, in this case, would create an absence of interest in the figure of an eschatological judge and in the conception of one who saves by being 'given up'. We are suggesting, in other words, that as Gnosticism fully developed it inclined to turn away from the presentation of the Son of Man as found in the canonical Gospels and thus either to omit it or to transform it (and/or to transform a usage which had been inherited from earlier Christian or from non-Christian thought).

There are several other second-century uses of the Son of Man which stand in close relation to synoptic materials, but they are few and far between.[107] One may quote from fragment 35 of Heracleon preserved for us in Origen's *Commentary on John* where some relationship with Matt. 13.37, 39 is evident, as is also the gnostic redaction. 'The Son of Man (υἱὸς ἀνθρώπου) above the Place sows; the saviour, who is himself also Son of Man (υἱὸς ἀνθρώπου), reaps and sends the angels known through the disciples, each for his own soul.'[108] The gnostic conception of two Sons of Man puzzled even Origen, but we could recognize an association with older gnostic understandings which we have already discussed. Here, however, the dual conception may rely more directly on the Matthean statements which would readily lend themselves to such a view.

[106] Neither does Thomas, log. 86, lend any support to the theory that this synoptic logion was based on a misunderstanding of Aramaic idiom. *pshēre mprōme* is the standard articular form found in almost all Coptic references.

[107] See also *Excerpta ex Theodoto* 4.3 and 61.4 (R. P. Casey, *The Excerpta ex Theodoto of Clement of Alexandria* [Studies and Documents I], London 1934), which apparently make use of a version of Matt. 16.28 and of the Son of Man passion tradition respectively.

[108] Quoted from R. M. Grant, *Gnosticism: an Anthology*, London 1961, 203. Cf. A. E. Brooke, *The Fragments of Heracleon* (Texts and Studies I, 4), Cambridge 1891, for the text.

There are three references to the Son of Man in the treatise 'On the Resurrection' (CG I/3) otherwise known as 'The Epistle to Rheginos'. Since this work, though employing gnostic terminology, stands considerably closer to non-gnostic Christian understandings[109] than most other works found at Nag Hammadi, it is probably not surprising that the references to the Son of Man are seemingly more in keeping with the kind of development that we might have expected in early Christianity. Though none of the statements about the Son of Man appear to be directly dependent upon canonical materials, they do speak of the resurrection in language like that found in the Gospels, and they do take up the themes concerning the resurrection[110] and the saviour's humanity which were also used in connection with the Son of Man in non-gnostic Christian writings of this period.

The first use of the designation in this treatise is interesting in that we find an anarthrous form which is unusual if not unique in the Coptic. We are at first reminded of the anarthrous usage in Ignatius' *To the Ephesians* 20.2 and *Barnabas* 12.10, where the designation could seem more of a description with reference to Jesus' humanity than a title of dignity.[111] In this case, however, the designation clearly has titular nuance, and the usage would seem to have been controlled by grammatical considerations, since the second of the references to the designation but seven lines later has the articles. Also in 44.29 we find *nshēre nnoute*, i.e. Son of God without the articles.[112]

---

[109] The view of Puech and Quispel that the treatise is an early Valentinian writing, quite possibly by Valentinus himself, has now been subjected to extensive criticism by Peel (*Rheginos*, 156ff.), who himself suggests that the work is a product of the last quarter of the second century, composed by an anonymous Valentinian-Christian who was in the process of having his Valentinian views 're-Christianized'. Our quotations from the treatise are drawn from the English translation in the critical edition of M. Malinine, H.-C. Puech, G. Quispel, W. Till, R. McL. Wilson and J. Zandee, *De Resurrectione (Epistula ad Rheginum)*, Zürich/Stuttgart 1963, though we have accepted several of Peel's suggestions.

[110] Compare the two statements attributed to James, the Lord's brother, above 49ff.

[111] See again pp. 37ff. above, and especially p. 38 n. 24 on other comparable uses referring to the humanity.

[112] See also, for example, at 44.15f. and cf. Peel, *op. cit.*, 57f., 60. The editors of *De Resurrectione* (viii), with regard to other features of the dialect, find it 'remarkable that in expressions such as "Son of God", "Son of Man" the articles may also be omitted with the genitive when the expression is indeterminate'. This is probably not so remarkable if one recognizes that both

Now the
Son of God, Rheginos, was
(also) Son of Man,[113] and
he encompassed them
both, since he possessed
the manhood and the deity,
in order that on the one hand he might vanquish
death[114] through his being
Son of God,
and that on the other hand through the Son of
Man the restoration
to the Pleroma
might take place, because at
first he was from above,
a seed of the truth, when this
structure had not yet come into being.

(On the Resurrection, 44.21–36)

Line 26 with lines 22–23 would appear to present us with a form
of chiasmus, since all seem agreed that the author intended to
relate the mention of the Son of Man to the saviour's humanity.[115]
It is also clear, however, from lines 30–36 that the author com-
prehended more than mere humanity when he used the Son of
Man designation. The author is building on much larger understandings when he speaks of the Son of Man's work in restoration
to the Pleroma and when he notes that the Son of Man is from
above and pre-existent. He would seem to be suggesting that there
was an aspect of the pre-existent, upper world saviour which was
human-like. (Indeed, our author believes that all which is truly
human, as opposed to the flesh which is assumed in the lower
world, was pre-existent in the world above.)[116] The saviour, who
is the seed[117] of the truth (or Truth) is then able through his own

---

designations could be used this way in the Greek which the Subakhmimic is
certainly rendering. Compare John 5.27 and also John 10.36; 19.7 on which
see *SMMH*, 293.

[113] *pshē/re nde mpnoute rhēgine/neushēre nrōme.*

[114] Compare 46.18f. (quoted below) and 45.14f. On biblical parallels for
this language cf. Peel, *op. cit.*, 67, 78, 121. Compare also Odes of Sol. 15.9.

[115] Cf. *De Resurrectione* xxviii and Peel, *op. cit.*, 38, 59. Peel (61) points out
that the order is then reversed again in lines 27–33.

[116] Cf. 46.35–47.8. See Peel, *op. cit.*, 111f.

[117] σπέρμα. A frequent gnostic image. One should compare the reference
to 'the seed (σπέρμα) of the Son of Man' in Gospel of Philip 124.2, though
there used rather differently. See above, p. 80.

resurrection to establish the process by which all that is truly human and which also came down from above may be restored[118] to the Pleroma. He can do this because as the one who is also Son of God he is powerful over death.

This represents a forceful and comprehensive viewpoint which, we would contend, controls the wording here far more than does a background of language and ideas to be found in the Fourth Gospel. Although John's Gospel does think of the Son of Man as pre-existent and as having ascended to where he was before (John 6.62)[119] and, while it is proper to draw our attention to John 5.25–29 where the titles Son of Man and Son of God are closely associated in a context which is concerned with the arising of the dead,[120] it is also true that our author employs none of the distinctive Johannine vocabulary or imagery which are found in these passages. We would maintain, therefore, that, although the author could be indirectly influenced by understandings found in the Fourth Gospel, his phraseology here is actually fully under the control of his own distinctive interpretation of the salvation process. In this sense he has chosen to use the designation Son of Man, not merely as another title for the saviour,[121] but because of the nuances which enabled him to delineate the process for the restoration to the Pleroma of gnostic humanity.

The third of the references in Rheginos is uncommon in that it speaks of the Son of Man in a context with credal overtones, a setting for the Son of Man which is difficult to parallel in other material from the first and second centuries AD.

[118] On ἀποκατάστασις and other vocabulary of a gnostic character in this passage, cf. the notes of *De Resurrectione*, 23f. In the 'semi-realized' eschatology of our author the restoration has replaced the last day and the parousia.

[119] There is a better comparison with 44.34 in John 8.23, where Jesus says, 'I am from above'. Here, however, there is no mention of the Son of Man, at least not until 8.27.

[120] Cf. Peel, *op. cit.*, 61. What is explicitly referred to the Son of Man in John 5.27, however, is his authority to execute judgment. Peel also draws attention to Matt. 16.13, 16, where the two titles are associated, though there is no further basis for comparison. Peel notes, too (*op. cit.*, 60), that 'Son of Man' and 'Son of God' are found together in Odes of Sol. 36.3, though we would suggest a non-titular understanding of the anarthrous 'son of man' there and interpret the verse in a different sense. Cf. *SMMH*, 199.

[121] In this measure we would further qualify Peel's contention (*op. cit.*, 124) that the titles of the saviour in this treatise 'are in part synonymous and to a degree interchangeable'.

> For we came to know the Son of
> Man, and we came to believe (πιστεύειν)
> that he arose from the
> dead, and this is he of whom we say
> that he became the destruction
> of death, as it is a great one
> on whom they believe (πιστεύειν).
>
> (On the Resurrection, 46.14–20)

Many texts of John 9.35 do tell of believing *in* the Son of Man, but the context there has nothing to do with resurrection and there is no other sign of relationship with this passage. We may also notice that in lines 4–21 of page 46 the author uses πιστεύειν or πίστις eight times,[122] and on this basis we may suspect that the phraseology here is largely the author's own composition.

It is, on the other hand, evident that the author is echoing traditional Christian language when he speaks of the arising from the dead. In particular there is a strong parallel with Mark 9.9 which looks forward to the time when 'the Son of Man should have risen from the dead', and there are, of course, a number of other predictions in the Gospels which foretell the arising of the Son of Man on the third day. It is also true, however, that references to Jesus rising from the dead became basic to the Easter proclamation (cf. Matt. 28.7) and Christian teaching generally without reference to any particular title.[123] Since it is again true that our author elsewhere in this treatise makes no attempt to quote directly from New Testament materials, one may suspect that the reason for the occurrence of the Son of Man designation in 46.14f. in conjunction with 'he arose from the dead' in 46.16f. is due not to a recollection of a logion like Mark 9.9, but is instead occasioned by the author's desire to allude again to the understandings developed with reference to the title in 44.30–33.

The first portion of the work known as the Gospel of Mary contains two references to the Son of Man which, though they again do not reveal a specific connection with any Son of Man

[122] Interestingly the author never uses the words elsewhere in the treatise. Peel (*op. cit.*, 131) rightly points out that what is really surprising here is the grounding of this belief in historical event. Such historical interest is rarely found in writings under the influence of Gnosticism.

[123] Compare this author's statement about the saviour having 'raised himself up' in 45.19.

tradition recorded in the canonical Gospels, do, none the less, give the distinct impression of some relationship with tradition now found in the synoptics. Jesus has made a resurrection appearance and is now engaged in his parting address to his disciples.

> When the Blessed One had said this, he
> greeted them all and said:
> Peace (be) unto you. Receive you
> my peace. Beware that no one
> leads you astray with the words:
> 'See here!' or 'See
> there!' For the Son of Man
> is within you. Follow
> after him! Those who seek him, shall
> find him. Go, therefore, and preach
> the Gospel of the kingdom. I have
> issued no command other than that
> which I appointed for you. Nor have I
> given any law like the lawgiver, that
> you may not be constrained thereby.
>
> (Gospel of Mary, BG 8502, 8.12–9.5)[124]

The central portion of this passage represents an amalgam of references from the canonical Gospels or the traditions on which they are based; such passages as John 14.27;[125] 20.19, 21, 26; Matt. 4.23; 7.7; 9.35; 24.5, 23; Mark 13.5, 21 and Luke 17.21 all come into consideration. The parallel which most interests us is, of course, Luke 17.21. Beginning with 17.20b we read: 'The kingdom of God is not coming with signs to be observed; nor will they say, "Lo, here it is!" or "There!" for behold, the kingdom of God is within (*or*, in the midst of) you.' Other gnostics were certainly able to make use of such language, as is evident from Gospel of Thomas, logion 3,[126] and from Naassene materials.[127] It

[124] W. C. Till, *Die gnostischen Schriften des koptischen Papyrus Berolinensis* 8502 (TU 60), 1955.

[125] On this declaration of peace by the risen Jesus cf. also Sophia of Jesus Christ, BG 8502, 79.10–12.

[126] The reference to the kingdom also being 'without you' (so Thomas, log. 3) is not found in Oxyrhynchus Papyrus 654, ii. On the interpretation of this logion, cf. Gärtner, *Theology of Thomas*, 213ff. See also the somewhat different use of Luke 17.21 in Thomas, log. 113. Gärtner points, too, to the Manichaean Psalmbook, 160.20f.

[127] Hippolytus, *Refut*. V.7.20.

well suited their understandings to conceive of a kingdom that was an inner reality[128] with no outward phenomena.

We might suppose, then, that such an understanding of an inner kingdom was brought into close association with a reference to the Son of Man. Indeed, references to the Son of Man do stand in Luke 17.22ff., and we can also point to the mention of 'the gospel of the kingdom' in Gospel of Mary 8.22, to be followed by 'the gospel of the kingdom of the Son of Man' in 9.9f. The conceptions could be as closely related as this, so that the kingdom is viewed as the possession of the Son of Man and, apparently, so that the Son of Man could even replace reference to the kingdom in a version of Luke 17.21.

Further motivation for the formation of such a saying could have been supplied by the gnostic belief that men below could be representative of the Man and/or Son of Man above[129] in terms either of the image or the divine spark within each individual. In whatever way the saying was, in fact, formed, this certainly would have been a way of interpreting 'the Son of Man is within you'.[130]

It is just possible on our view, however, that, apart from the question of interpretation, the author of this Gospel has not composed the saying, but is rather dependent here on earlier materials. If Luke 17.20f. can be regarded as largely a Lucan creation, and, if the author of Mary had some access to materials which lay behind our Gospels, then it will be necessary to take Luke 17.23 into consideration: 'And they shall say to you "Lo, there! Lo, here!" Go not away, nor follow after.' In a similar tradition in Matthew and Mark[131] a search for the Christ is made the subject for this vain looking. In both Matthew (24.26; for the second time) and Luke, however, the pericope occurs in the context of a Q passage where again the great concern is with how one awaits a *figure* (rather than a 'conception' like the kingdom), in particular the Son of Man. Because of the respect which one must give to the Q material and as a result of our understanding that a concern with the Christ and the kingdom has elsewhere influenced materials

---

[128] So *mpetnhoun* (similarly the Sahidic of Luke 17.21 and Thomas, log. 3) apparently interprets Luke's ambiguous Greek ἐντὸς ὑμῶν (so also in P. Oxy. 654, ii, line 16).

[129] See above, pp. 73f., on the Naassenes, and compare the Gospel of Philip's 'son of the Son of Man', perhaps a closely related idea.

[130] Similarly Gärtner, *op. cit.*, 216.

[131] Matt. 24.23; Mark 13.21.

whose original concern was with the Son of Man, we are willing to ask if this 'Lo, here! . . . Lo, there!'[132] language might not, in an earlier form, have had to do with the Son of Man expectation. We may also notice, for purposes of our comparison, that a synoptic passage with a rather similar import uses the words 'Take heed that no man leads you astray'.[133] In this same pericope in Luke's version we also find the words 'Do not go after them'.

Nor can there be overlooked a curious feature which is part of the Matthean (Q) parallel. Commentators have often been puzzled by the 'Lo, he is in the inner rooms' (ἐν τοῖς ταμιείοις) of Matt. 24.26. We might surmise that this, too, represents an attempt to interpret some earlier reference to 'within' in the original saying. Just possibly Matthew has here caught the primitive thought better than the others.

Making use of the several traditions in a way which would give us the best parallel to the Gospel of Mary logion, we may make the following comparisons.

Hypothetical Synoptic Tradition (Luke 17.23 amended)	*Gospel of Mary* (BG 8502 8.14–20)	*Luke 17.21*	*Matt. 24.26*
(Take heed that no man leads you astray.)	Beware that no one leads you astray		So, if they
They will say to you: 'Lo here!'	with the words: 'See here!'	Nor will they say: 'Lo, here it is!'	say to you: 'Lo, he is in the wilderness, do not go out.'
or 'Lo there	or 'See there!' For	or 'There.' For, behold,	If they say, 'Lo
he (the Son of Man)	the Son of Man	the kingdom of God	he
is among (within?) (you?)'	is within you.	is among (within) you.	is in the inner rooms,'
Do not go, do not follow ( )!	Follow after him!		do not believe it.

Luke 17.24 (= Matt. 24.27): For as the lightning flashes and lights up the sky from one side to the other, so will the Son of Man be (in his day).

[132] So the Marcan word order, perhaps suggested also by Matthew. So, too, Thomas, log. 113.
[133] Mark 13.5; Matt. 24.4; Luke 21.8.

The tradition represented by our amended Luke 17.23 would then have become sufficiently popular as a way of speaking so as to have become loosened from its context in the sequence of Son of Man sayings. As a popular saying it sometimes gained a more positive thrust. In one line of tradition the reference to the Son of Man was either retained or made explicit. In another the figure of concern became the Christ. In yet another it was turned into a concern with the kingdom of God and into an understanding probably anomalous in the synoptic tradition,[134] however ἐντός is understood. Luke or his source then gave the saying a setting in a little apothegm story.[135]

It is not as evident that the second Son of Man logion in the Gospel of Mary is dependent on either synoptic or synoptic-related tradition, but there does seem again to be a measure of kinship. After Jesus has spoken his final words in the passage quoted above, he departs. The disciples then grieve and weep heavily, saying:

> How shall we
> go to the heathen (ἔθνος) and preach
> the gospel of the kingdom of the Son
> of Man? If he was not
> spared at all, how should we
> be spared?
>
> (Gospel of Mary, BG 8502, 9.7–12)

Mary Magdalene then tells the disciples not to weep, since his grace will be with them.

It is quite possible that, in this case, the expression 'the gospel of the kingdom of the Son of Man' originated within the tradition of this Gospel, perhaps out of the references to 'the Son of Man' and 'the gospel of the kingdom' spoken of by Jesus in lines 8.18 and 8.22. Indeed, this would seem most natural as the disciples here are apparently referring to Jesus' earlier statement that they should go and preach the 'gospel'.

The issue is, however, again complicated by the existence of references to the kingdom and the Son of Man in the *Sophia Jesu Christi* and the Letter of Eugnostos, two writings which, as we

---

[134] Otherwise understood and regarded as authentic by Perrin, *Rediscovering the Teaching of Jesus*, 68ff.

[135] So on the setting Bultmann, *History of the Synoptic Tradition*, 54f.

shall soon see, are at the least closely related to one another. In the Sophia (BG 8502, 101.6–7) we are told that 'the kingdom belongs to the Son of Man'. In Eugnostos (CG III, 81.12–14; not contained in the CG V version) we hear that 'the kingdom of the Son of Man is full of indescribable joy'. The problem of the derivation of such an understanding is made more difficult by the possibility, argued for by Martin Krause, that the Eugnostos letter is a non-Christian writing on which the *Sophia Jesu Christi* has built.

On the one hand, one can certainly argue that the conception of the Son of Man having a kingdom has grown directly from the understandings expressed in Matt. 16.28 ('There are some standing here who will not taste death before they see the Son of Man coming in his kingdom')[136] and Matt. 13.41 ('The Son of Man will send his angels, and they will gather out of his kingdom all causes of sin and all evildoers').[137] One can, however, also point behind Matthew to the 'one like a son of man' in Daniel who is given 'dominion, glory and kingdom' (*mal^ekū*); '. . . his kingdom shall not be destroyed'.[138] While I Enoch does not reproduce the conception as such, it certainly knows of a Son of Man who reigns from the very throne of God. It is, therefore, at least feasible that the conception of the Son of Man's kingdom was also known outside of Christian circles.[139]

For the idea of *preaching the gospel* of this kingdom, however, one naturally looks for specifically Christian parallels. One may point to the preaching of the gospel of the kingdom of God in some texts of Mark 1.14 or to preaching the gospel of the kingdom in Matt. 4.23. There are Pauline references to 'the gospel of his Son' (Rom. 1.9) and to 'the gospel of Christ'[140] and to preaching the gospel of Christ (II Cor. 2.12). The closest parallel in terms of both language and context is provided by Matt. 24.14: 'And this gospel of the kingdom will be preached throughout the whole world, as a testimony to all nations' (ἔθνος). Our passage from the Gospel of Mary, however, indicates direct dependence upon none of these.

We might wish that the opening six pages of this Gospel were

136 On Matt. 16.28 see above, pp. 21f.
137 Compare also Matt. 25.31.
138 Dan. 7.13f.
139 Cf. also below, pp. 117ff., on the man/son of man and Gen. 1.26 along with Ps. 8.4ff., where, in both cases, the man is given 'dominion'.
140 I Cor. 9.12; II Cor. 9.13; 10.14; Gal. 1.7; Phil. 1.27; I Thess. 3.2.

extant. There is every indication that the first nine pages composed a separate work[141] which at some time was knit together with the latter section. It is only this second section which would appropriately have borne the title 'the Gospel of Mary'.[142] If this analysis of our text is correct, we then have two references to the Son of Man in the last three pages of a single gnostic work, and one must wonder about the contents of the first six pages.

There are six references to the Son of Man in the *Sophia Jesu Christi*, and the problems occasioned by the title's employment in the work are, as we have already begun to see, severely compounded by the relation of this Sophia of Jesus Christ to the work known as the Epistle of Eugnostos.[143] Although Schenke and Till[144] have contended that Eugnostos represents a later de-Christianized version of the Christian gnostic Sophia, Martin Krause and others hold that the *Sophia Jesu Christi* is a Christianization of the earlier gnostic Eugnostos.[145] Indeed, this is viewed by Krause as representative of a process of Christianization which is visible in other of the Nag Hammadi writings, although in most

---

[141] R. McL. Wilson in 'The New Testament in the Gnostic Gospel of Mary', *NTS* 3, 1956/7, 236ff., also finds that 7.1–8.11 in this section could originally have been part of a non-Christian work.

[142] Cf. Puech in *NTA* I, 341. The response of Mary to the disciples' grief would likely have formed the connecting link. Puech (*op. cit.*, 344) contends that the whole work may be dated in the second century with some certainty.

[143] The *Sophia Jesu Christi* is the third work in BG 8502. There is a second version which is work 4 of CG III. Eugnostos is found in CG III/3 (there best preserved) and CG V/1. Since these Nag Hammadi versions are yet to be published at the time of writing, I am grateful to Professor Martin Krause for communicating directly to me with regard to significant passages. A German translation of Eugnostos will appear in 1970 in *Die Gnosis* Band II (Koptische und mandäische Texte eingeleitet, übersetzt und erläutert von M. Krause und K. Rudolph, Artemis-Verlag, Zürich und Stuttgart). There will also be a synopsis of the Coptic texts of the Sophia and Eugnostos in *Patristische Texte und Studien* and a German translation in *Kleine Texte für Vorlesungen und Übungen* from de Gruyter, Berlin.

[144] Schenke in 'Nag Hamadi Studien II: Das System der Sophia Jesu Christi', *ZRGG* 14, 1962, 263ff. See the summary of the discussion by J. M. Robinson, 'The Coptic Gnostic Library Today', *NTS* 14, 1967/8, 374f., with reference to Till, and also to the views of Quispel, Doresse and Puech, who stand closer to Krause. As Robinson points out, only Krause had, at this time, all the texts available to him.

[145] M. Krause, 'Das literarische Verhältnis des Eugnostosbriefes zur Sophia Jesu Christi. Zur Auseinandersetzung der Gnosis mit dem Christentum', *Mullus: Festschrift Theodor Klauser* (Jahrbuch für Antike und Christentum. Ergänzungsband 1, 1964: Münster), 215ff.

other cases we are not so fortunate as to have the *Vorlage* for the Christianized treatise.[146]

Krause maintains that there was originally a gnostic cosmogonic writing which was concerned to refute certain other philosophical views and to set forth its own theory regarding the nature of the universe. Essential to the work is the contention that the Propator-Autopator is totally unknowable and ineffable, altogether a pure intelligence which is proper to himself alone.[147] This God, however, in the process of knowing or seeing himself has an image as that of a Father which appears in the infinite. There thus is produced a great androgynous Man whose masculine name is lost to us but whose feminine name is Sophia-Pansophos. This immortal Man creates a great aeon. From him proceeds a son known as the Son of Man and who may also be called Protogenetor. He also belongs wholly to the upper world and his is the second aeon. This creator figure unites with his consort Sophia to reveal himself a great bisexual luminary whose masculine name is Saviour and whose feminine name is Sophia. From him proceed six other pairs and so the process of creation continues. This second 'son' is, however, said to have a clearly independent existence and his own aeon only in the version of Eugnostos found in Nag Hammadi Codex V. There it is maintained that his is the third great aeon, and he is styled the son of the Son of Man.

In Krause's view this basic treatise was at some point given epistolary trimmings and corresponding changes in style by the unknown author standing behind the programmatic name Eugnostos.[148] Doubtless this work was originally composed in Greek (as was the still later first version of the *Sophia Jesu Christi* from which there is extant a Greek fragment in P. Oxy. 1081). The popularity of this Epistle of Eugnostos, still non-Christian though showing obvious traces of Jewish influence, is suggested by the presence of the two versions at Nag Hammadi.

Krause believes that the Codex V version of Eugnostos stands

[146] See also Krause's 'Der Stand der Veröffentlichung der Nag Hammadi Texte' in *Le Origini dello Gnosticismo, Colloquio di Messina* 13–18 Aprile 1966 (Studies in the History of Religions, Supplements to Numen XII), Leiden 1967, 61ff.

[147] See also the summary account by J. Doresse, *The Secret Books of the Egyptian Gnostics*, ET, London 1960, 192ff.

[148] Of the so-called Gospel of the Egyptians (see below) it is said: 'He who transcribed it is Eugnostos, the agapite, in the spirit; in the flesh my name is Goggessos' (CG III, 69.10–12).

closest to the basic work. Here is maintained the clear structure of
three primary emanations identified with the first three aeons. In
V, 13.8–13 we are told that the first aeon belongs to the immortal
Man and the second to the Son of Man whom they call 'The
Firstborn'. Then there is the third aeon of this son of the Son of
Man who is an androgynous light from the Son of Man and his
consort Sophia. His manly name is 'Saviour'. In the parallel in the
Codex III version of Eugnostos (CG III, 85.8–14) we are told only
of two aeons, the first that of the immortal Man and the second
that of the Son of Man, whom they are accustomed to call Protogenetor and Saviour. Krause sees here a tendency to erode
distinctions of function, a process which is carried on with an
added measure of confusion in the Christianized Sophia. There, in
a parallel passage, we read:

> The Perfect Saviour
> said: 'He who
> has ears to hear, let him
> hear. The first aeon
> is that of the Son of Man
> whom one
> calls "Proto-
> genetor" (and) who (also)
> is called "the Saviour",
> who has appeared.
> The second aeon is that
> of the Man, whom one calls
> "Adam, the eye
> of light".'
>
> (BG 8502, 107.17–108.11)

Here, it would seem there has been an alteration in order, and
there is a further tendency, which Krause notes elsewhere, to
move the role of saviour to the highest position. One may surmise
that it was the identification of the Man with Adam which could
have caused a later writer to think of the first Man of the earth and
thus no longer to style him as 'immortal'. He is, then, positioned
below the upper world Son of Man. Earlier in the Sophia, however, the proper order (cf. also BG 8502, 98.15–99.12, on which
see below) and understanding of this specialized use of Adam
seems to be retained when the protogenetor-Father is called
'Adam, the eye of light' (BG 8502, 100.12f.). Even here, however,

the composer of the Sophia would seem to be attempting to give the Son of Man, who in this version is also called the Christ[149] (in the version of the Sophia CG III/4 he is called Son of God), a definite priority. After describing the kingdom of this 'Adam', the author insists: 'But the kingdom[150] belongs to the Son of Man'.[151] In the Eugnostos version of Codex III we also hear 'but the kingdom of the Son of Man is full of indescribable joy',[152] yet there seems no effort here specifically to exalt the role of the Son of Man above his place in the order of things. That the author of the Sophia may here be expanding on a statement known from Eugnostos is perhaps indicated by a comparison of the two parallel versions.

But the kingdom belongs to the Son of Man, whom one calls the Christ. There is completely full indescribable, shadowless joy and immutable exaltation. (BG 8502, 101.6–12)	But the kingdom of the Son of Man is full of indescribable joy. (CG III, 81.12–14)

In a passage containing the third of the references to the Son of Man found in both Eugnostos and the Sophia we may gain the distinct impression that knowledge of a third emanation (one from the Son of Man) was fundamental in a cosmogonic structure which has influenced the two writings. In the *Sophia Jesu Christi*'s version we read:[153]

> The Son
> of Man agreed with
> Sophia, his consort,
> and revealed himself in a
> [great light] as both male
> [and female. His] maleness
> is called

[149] Since the speaker is also addressed as the Christ (e.g. BG 8502, 99.4) and thus is made to speak of himself in the third person, the suspicion grows that the writer of the Sophia is working with earlier materials on to which he has imposed the question-answer structure.

[150] In the parallel in CG III/4 the polemical tone seems even stronger as it speaks of 'the whole kingdom'.

[151] BG 8502, 101.6f.

[152] CG III, 81.12–14. The statement is lacking in CG V/1. On the meaning of such a statement and on its relationship to a similar expression in the Gospel of Mary, see above, pp. 92f.

[153] The parallels from Eugnostos are found in CG III, 81.21ff. and CG V, 10.4ff.

'the Saviour,
the begetter of all things',
but his female nature
'Sophia, Mother of All',
whom some
call 'Pistis'.

(BG 8502, 102.15–103.9)

It would seem that the composer of this version of the Sophia has understood that the Son of Man 'revealed himself in (*hnn*) a great light', but the parallels in Eugnostos and in the Nag Hammadi version of the Sophia tell us that he 'revealed himself (*n-*) a (or, as a) great light', suggesting, in the gnostic manner of thought, another manifestation.

We are naturally reminded by this, not only of the references to the son of the Son of Man in the Gospel of Philip,[154] but also of the conception of Seth made 'in the image of the Son of Man' which is to be found in the Apocryphon of John.[155] If Krause is correct in his analysis of the relationship of the *Sophia Jesu Christi* to Eugnostos, we would at least need to be alert to the possibility that an extra-Christian cosmogonic view has caused these various sectarians to think in terms of a son of the Son of Man, which then has been fitted into a Christian-gnostic outlook.

Krause's method includes not only a study of the Christian elements (e.g. 'He who has ears to hear, let him hear' four times in the Sophia) and nuances (e.g. the explicit or implicit contention that the Saviour-Christ alone teaches all truth) which, he maintains, could have been added by the author of the Sophia, but also a comparison of the special material from each work with the material that is common to all four versions and is, therefore, basic. In these terms, much of the material peculiar to the Sophia is found to be incompatible with the basic material, while this is not true of the special material from Eugnostos. This understanding, Krause argues, is corroborated by other comparisons. The more congruous arrangement of material in the Epistle is in the Sophia broken up to fit into a pattern of questions and answers between

---

[154] See above, pp. 78ff.
[155] See below, pp. 109f. One might also compare Monoïmus's teaching (above, p. 71) that the Son of Man sends *rays* down on the world. If there is a legitimate comparison here, it seems to represent a conception more like that of the BG version of the Sophia.

the disciples and the Saviour, such as is found in other Christian-gnostic works.[156] The questions do not always well correspond to the answers drawn out of the common material,[157] and other special materials of a Christian character also break up passages which can be seen to belong together.

Krause's careful analysis cannot be said to exhaust all the possibilities, and the relationships between these several texts may yet be found to be more complicated. The implications of the possibilities he has articulated are, however, important for our study. In all the other works we have studied or are to study Christian influences may be seen to be present. While references to the Son of Man (and especially to the Man and the Son of Man) do at times occur in contexts which do not appear to be specifically Christian, it is always possible to argue that the mention of the Son of Man is, none the less, an indication of Christian influence. If, however, Krause is correct in maintaining that the Epistle of Eugnostos represents non-Christian thought which only later came to be Christianized, then we have at least one instance of a non-Christian usage of the term in Gnosticism for which we might well need to seek another source than Christianity. Although one can argue that the designation itself was yet borrowed from Christianity, this might seem like special pleading unless other specifically Christian features can be identified.[158] In our concluding remarks we shall attempt to indicate other possible sources for the use of Man/Son of Man language in extra-Christian gnostic thought.

There remain the three other references to the Son of Man in the *Sophia Jesu Christi* which are not found in Eugnostos and which, therefore, on Krause's thesis, probably ought to be attributed to the writer of the Sophia. It is, of course, feasible that he has borrowed one or more of them from the material basic to both Eugnostos and his treatise, which the former made no use of, but, upon examination, all seem readily accounted for as the product of

[156] Here Krause's view (in *Mullus*, 220) is in contrast to that of Schenke ('Nag Hamadi Studien II', 265), who finds it scarcely credible that anyone would have broken up the more systematized presentation of the Eugnostos letter, while a later systematization of material first presented in terms of questions and answers is quite credible.

[157] Cf. also p. 97 n. 149 above.

[158] Krause (in *Mullus*, 215 n. 18) points out that Schenke had so far not enumerated such features.

the editorial work of the Sophia's composer, striving to give a semblance of unity to his work.

The very first of the references to the Son of Man in the treatise is found in a question placed on the lips of Bartholomew: 'How was he in the Gospel called "the Man" and "the Son of Man"? From which of them is this Son?' (BG 8502, 98.9–13). The answer of the Holy One which follows (98.15–99.12) tells of the First Man who reflects with Sophia and causes his protogenetor to appear as a bisexual child. The male name is Protogenetor, Son of God; he is the Christ. The female name is Urmother, Sophia, Mother of All. We have here, in other words, an answer which closely approximates the story of an emanation of the Son of Man or the creation of another 'son' by the Son of Man as it is related in BG 8502, 102.15–103.9 and the parallels in the versions of Eugnostos. It is surprising only in that the designation Son of Man is not found in the answer, but in the question. The existence of these other accounts and the fact that the title is found in the question furthers our suspicion that the author has borrowed the title from the materials which he used to compose the answer. He thus apparently attempted to make firm the understanding that the one otherwise called the Son of Man is also the Christ, the Son of God.

Indeed, Bartholomew's question may suggest that, not only the fictionalized disciple, but also the author of the Sophia was having some difficulty understanding an earlier teaching about the Man and the Son of Man. In this sense 'the Gospel' mentioned here could refer to the Eugnostos letter (or some work on which both are based) or, more probably, to the general stock of belief and tradition in which both titles are found closely linked.[159]

Near the end of the Sophia the author, in his closing exhortation, presents two final references to the Son of Man:

> He who apprehends
> the Son of Man
> in understanding and
> love should
> bring to me a sign (σύμβολον)

[159] 'The Man' as a title is, of course, not found in the canonical Gospels. Otherwise it is at least possible that Bartholomew is referring to the Gospel of Philip or the so-called Gospel of the Egyptians (see below), where both titles are joined.

of[160] the Son of Man,
and he will be[161] at
that place with those who
are in the Ogdoad.

(BG 8502, 124.1–9)

It is conceivable that there is a passing reference to Matt. 24.30 and the sign ($\sigma\eta\mu\epsilon\hat{\iota}o\nu$) of the Son of Man there, although the two signs seem of a very different kind with different functions to perform. In the case of the Sophia it is likely that some formula or password was in mind. In any event, the passage can with some safety be regarded as part of a summary by the author, picking up the title which he had made use of, in the last instance, some sixteen pages earlier.

The Apocryphon of John presents us with issues which are also complicated by different versions of the work. In this case, however, all four texts bear a definite Christian-gnostic stamp, although again Krause would contend that the Christian elements can be identified as secondary and as additions to a fundamentally gnostic piece of literature.[162] Our use of the four versions is simplified to some extent by the fact that BG 8502/2 and CG III/1 are directly comparable as 'short' versions, while CG II/1 and the less well-preserved CG IV/1 are 'long' versions.[163] Although the majority of scholars appear to regard the short version as 'more primitive', Søren Giversen presents a detailed argument for seeing the short version as derived from the long.[164] At the present time no firm decision on the matter seems possible, and it may well turn out that the relationship between the long and short versions is not to be explained only by regarding one as secondary to the other. Both versions may preserve elements from a yet earlier version or versions.

Fortunately, however, for the sake of our study of one of the most important episodes in gnostic lore, all four versions of the

---

[160] The version in CG III reads 'from the Son of Man'.

[161] The version in CG III reads 'he will go to that place . . .'

[162] Krause, 'Der Stand der Veröffentlichung der Nag Hammadi Texte', *Le Origini dello Gnosticismo*, 75. See also Sasuga Arai, 'Zur Christologie des Apokryphons des Johannes', *NTS* 15, 1968/9, 302ff.

[163] The three Nag Hammadi versions in *Die drei Versionen des Apokryphon des Johannes im koptischen Museum zu Alt-Kairo*, M. Krause and P. Labib, Wiesbaden 1962.

[164] *Apocryphon Johannis. The Coptic Text of the Apocryphon Johannis in the Nag Hammadi Codex II with Translation, Introduction and Commentary* (Acta Theologica Danica V), Copenhagen 1963.

Apocryphon do preserve the incident of the demiurge's blasphemy and the reply to it in rather similar parallel forms. The essentials of the basic story, which occurs in a number of gnostic writings, seem regularly to include the begetting of the powers of the upper heavens through a series of emanations originating from the unknowable Father of All. One of these emanations is Sophia, or Pistis, who commits the folly of trying to create without help from her partner. The result is the powerful but miscreant god frequently known as Ialdabaoth, but also as Saclas, Samael[165] as well as the Archigenetor, Protarchon and other such designations. In much of the mythological interpretation he is regarded as the God known in the Jewish scriptures, he who in relative ignorance made the 'lower' heavens and who later behaves in despotic ways toward human creatures.

After Ialdabaoth has made the created heavens with its denizens, he looks about and in his folly boasts that he alone is God and that there is no other beside him.[166] Sometimes, however, preceding this blasphemy we are told, in varying degrees of detail, of the repentance and sorrow of Sophia with regard to her misbegetting. She pleads for assistance from her fellow emanation or emanations, but is given only partial help from the Spirit or Holy Spirit. That portion of the upper light world which passed from her to the lower world or chaos will eventually be redeemed, but, for the time being, a veil is drawn between the upper and lower worlds and Sophia must remain in the upper of the lower heavens, that is, in the realm of Ialdabaoth. It is at this point that Ialdabaoth's blasphemy occurs.

A voice is then sounded by means of which Ialdabaoth hears that he is in grave error and by which he also often learns that Man, or Man and the Son of Man, existed before him. The source and primary purpose of this utterance are variously reported in different versions. Usually it issues from the upper world, though several times the words are spoken by Pistis herself and once by her

---

[165] He 'has now three names: the first name is Ialdabaoth, the second is Saclas, the third is Samael', Apocryphon of John, CG II, 11.15–18 = CG IV, 17.25–18.2. Not found in the 'short' versions. On the interpretation of these names, cf. A. Böhlig, 'Der jüdische und judenchristliche Hintergrund in gnostischen Texten von Nag Hammadi' in *Le Origini dello Gnosticismo*, 115f.

[166] The various gnostic statements are at least closely related to Isa. 44.6; 45.5f.; 46.9 (cf. Ex. 20.3). The motif of a 'jealous God' is sometimes included; see Ex. 20.5; 34.14; Deut. 5.9.

daughter Zoe. Sometimes the utterance acts as a kind of confirmation and consolation for Sophia, which Ialdabaoth overhears; at other times it is a direct rebuke to this blasphemer.

Next, either as an immediate sequel to this voice or in response to Ialdabaoth's disbelief of its message, there is glimpsed in the waters of the lower world a reflection of the image of the celestial Man whose pre-existence has been proclaimed. Enamoured of its beauty, the demiurge and/or his followers model an earthly man. Either due to the image in which he was created or because of a subsequent gift of spiritual power from the upper world (though on occasion only Eve seems to have this gift), it is understood that *man* (and hence mankind or some portion of mankind) possesses a refraction from the upper world of light. There then follow various gnostic interpretations of the story of Eden and the ensuing chapters of Genesis. In several of these narratives it is through Seth, the son of Adam, the first man, that the race of those who are to be saved is traced. Colouring the interpretations there is recognizable the gnostic faith that true men must avoid the error of worshipping the creator-god, awake to their heritage from the upper world and thus eventually return their portion of this light world to its genuine home.

The popularity of this general myth is revealed not only by its many retellings by differing gnostic groups, but also by the variety of modifications and additions to the story, somewhat bewildering to us, but attesting to the importance of the myth to those who wrote or copied it over and again. Indeed, even in cases where we do not hear of the Sophia's misbegetting of the demiurge or of his blasphemy, the outline of other portions of such a mythological interpretation of the Genesis account are clearly discernible. Thus, in the myth of the Poimandres we also hear of a heavenly Man, made by the high God, who reflects his image of God in the water below and, coming to love it, unites with it to form a creature of two natures.[167] In this case certainly, and probably just as certainly in the case of the more extensive myth which we have sketched in above, we are dealing with fundamental gnostic and originally non-Christian speculation which reaches back toward the very roots of gnostic lore and discloses clear dependence upon and an intimate relation with a form or forms of Jewish faith and tradition.

[167] Cf. *Corpus Hermeticum* I.12–15.

The question which is once more our particular concern asks about the place of the Son of Man in that line of tradition which also regularly tells of Ialdabaoth's blasphemy. In all of these cases we are dealing with materials which are now Christian-gnostic, though in every instance the question can and has legitimately been raised as to whether we are not working with traditions which have secondarily been Christianized. Whether found in originally Christian or secondarily Christianized writings, however, we still would wish to know whether the mention of the Son of Man should be attributed to Christian influence or whether it can better be traced to Jewish influenced gnostic thought.

In the 'long' version of the Apocryphon we are given two renderings of the demiurge's claim to be God alone. In the first of these, after his own creation and activity in creating other aeons, Ialdabaoth looks about, and, in his ungodly ignorance of the source of his own strength and the place from which he had come, he exults: 'I am God, and there is no other God but me.'[168] This statement, in that there is no explicit mention of his jealousy and because it does not tell us that the claim was made to his angels, bears comparison with versions of the blasphemy found in other cosmogonic works, the Hypostasis of the Archons ('I [am] God; there is none [beside me]'[169] and 'I am God, and there is no other beside me'[170] as well as 'I am God of all'[171]) and in the closely related Treatise without a Title ('I am God, and no other exists besides me'[172] and 'I am God; there is no other beside me'[173]). Each of these utterances from the Hypostasis and the untitled treatise leads or is directly related to a rebuke telling the demiurge (three times called Samael, explained as meaning 'the blind god', and once Saclas), 'You do err'.[174] In only one instance, however, does the voice (that of Pistis herself) go on to explain that 'an immortal light Man exists before you',[175] although both treatises are well aware of the story of the creation of the first

---

[168] See CG II, 11.18–22 = CG IV, 18.2–6 (badly preserved).

[169] CG II, 86.30f. Cf. J. Leipoldt and H.-M. Schenke, *Koptisch-gnostische Schriften aus den Papyrus-Codices von Nag-Hamadi*, 69ff.

[170] CG II, 94.21f.

[171] CG II, 95.5.

[172] CG II, 103.12f. See below, p. 107 n. 184.

[173] CG II, 107.30f.

[174] See CG II, 87.3f.; 94.25f.; 95.7f.; 103.17f.

[175] In the Treatise without a Title, CG II, 103.19f. Ialdabaoth is said to recognize the truth of this statement, CG II, 107.26f.

earthly man resulting from the reflection of an image of the high God in the waters below.

This first blasphemy proclaimed by Ialdabaoth in the Apocryphon of John also has a near parallel in the report of Irenaeus. Again there is no mention of his jealousy, and the cry is not directed to his angels. 'I am father and God, and above me there is no one,' he exclaims.[176]

The second blasphemy in the 'long' version of the Apocryphon (following the description of more creative work by Ialdabaoth and his archons) is closely paralleled in wording and context by the 'short' version. Surveying his creation and the multitude of his angels, Ialdabaoth maintains, 'I, I am a jealous God, and there is no other God but me.'[177] The versions then perceptively remark that Ialdabaoth thus reveals at least some awareness of another God, since why otherwise would he be jealous. (It is possible, however, that this commentary misses the point of an earlier understanding, that Ialdabaoth was jealous even toward the powers he had created.)

In the Gospel of the Egyptians (or 'the Holy Book of the Great Invisible Spirit') Sacla said to his angels, 'I, I am a [jealous] God, and apart from me no other [exists—being (thus) dis]obedient to his hypostasis.'[178] We may also compare what Irenaeus has recorded in *Against Heresies* I.29.4, 'I am a jealous God, and besides me there is no one.' Here, however, it is not said that the demiurge addressed his cry to the angels, and Irenaeus, in this case, does not go on to report any retort to the blasphemy.[179]

While, in the case of the versions of the blasphemy recorded by Irenaeus in *Against Heresies* I.30.6, in the Gospel of the Egyptians, in the untitled treatise (CG II, 103.12f.) and all three times in

[176] *Adv. Haer.* I.30.6.

[177] CG II, 13.8f. = IV, 20.22–4. BG 8502, 44.14f. reads: 'I am a jealous God; beside me there is no other.' The statement is lacking in CG III, as pages 19 and 20 are missing.

[178] CG III, 58.24–59.1. There is another version of this work in CG IV/2. We make use here of Doresse's text and translation of CG III/2 in 'Le Livre Sacré du Grand Esprit Invisible' ou 'L'Évangile des Égyptiens', *JA* 254, 1966 317ff.

[179] It is strongly suspected that Irenaeus may be using a version, perhaps early, of the Apocryphon of John at this point. At least he is using a closely related source. He does not, however, report any anthropogonic material. Probably this is because there is much of a comparable character which he will use in his next chapter. Cf. Puech, *NTA* I, 317.

the Hypostasis of the Archons, the rebuking voice follows immediately, in all versions of the Apocryphon we are told first of Sophia's repentance over what she has wrought. (Compare with this the untitled treatise at CG II, 103.15f. where Pistis replies directly to the demiurge in anger. Similar seems the mother's motivation in *Against Heresies* I.30.6.)

In the untitled treatise Pistis responds, 'You do err, Samael . . . An immortal light Man exists before you.' He will be revealed in Samael's creation and trample him down like pottery clay.[180] In Irenaeus's report (I.30.6) the response is again given by Ialdabaoth's mother, but this time as 'Do not lie, Ialdabaoth, for the father of all, the first Man, is above thee, and Man the Son of Man.' In the other texts, where a comparable retort is given, the 'You do err' is also missing, a mention of the Son of Man is also included, but the voice is said to have come not from the mother (though in the Apocryphon Ialdabaoth is said to have believed that it did) but from the high heaven or aeon. In the Apocryphon it is also maintained that the voice was directed to the mother herself.

In all four versions of the Apocryphon and in the Gospel of the Egyptians[181] the words of the voice are identical: 'There exists Man and the Son of Man.'[182] The Apocryphon, like the version of the myth in Irenaeus I.30.6 and as in the untitled treatise, along with the Gospel of the Egyptians, then proceeds immediately to the creation of the first earthly man. In all versions except that found in Irenaeus this is said to be accomplished according to the image ($\epsilon i \kappa \omega \nu$)[183] or form of the celestial Man.

In setting out the versions of this basic story of blasphemy and the response to it we have taken the trouble to make mention of a measure of the attendant details in order to indicate the variety of ways by which the several accounts might be compared and categorized: by the name of the demiurge or his mother, by the context of the blasphemy and its wording, by the relation of the retort to the blasphemy, or by the source, purpose and form of

[180] CG II, 103.17–23.

[181] In the Gospel of the Egyptians (CG III, 59.2–4) only the conjunction and the form of the genitive prefix are different.

[182] The Apocryphon = CG II, 14.14f.; III, 21.17f.; IV, 22.17f.; BG 8502, 47.14–16.

[183] So in the Gospel of the Egyptians (CG III, 59.4) and the Apocryphon 'long' versions CG II, 14.21; IV, 22.25f.; in the Apocryphon 'short' versions CG III, 22.5; BG 8502, 48.9f.

the retort. Certain comparisons are possible, and we might suppose, for instance, that the primitive story closely associated the blasphemy with the response to it. Yet, of course, later reworkings could still make use of older wordings, and we unfortunately do not find that such comparisons can lead us to any definite conclusions regarding the relationships of these materials which will be useful for our purposes. Indeed, suggestions held out by one set of comparisons seem readily contradicted by others. This does, however, at least point us once more to the realization that we are working with a basic mythological scene which has been told and retold, in some cases the retellings having also influenced one another, though now it seems impossible to retrace these stages.

We must return, therefore, to our specific question about the place of the Son of Man in these traditions. Should the statement about the immortal light Man's existence, because it is shorter and there seems no obvious reasons why the mention of the Son of Man should have been omitted, be regarded as primary, even though outnumbered by the statements in the Apocryphon, the Gospel of the Egyptians and Irenaeus' report? In the light of such comparative materials as the Poimandres, which refer only to the heavenly Man and his image, this might seem the correct course. Reference to the Son of Man could then be regarded as the result of Christian influence at some stage in the transmission and use of this basic story.

On the other hand, some weight must be given to the preponderance of the versions which do speak of the Son of Man. However we attempt to date the untitled treatise, it itself has been subject to a number of interpolations and revisions[184] (as has also the closely related Hypostasis of the Archons), and it is at least conceivable that the mention of the Son of Man has been dropped because it was thought to be redundant and immaterial to the narrative as understood by a narrator or copyist at this point. Added to this we must remember that all the Coptic documents were copied or translated and copied no earlier than the fourth century. The Greek version of Irenaeus, therefore, written no later than AD 185, obviously has a kind of priority.[185]

[184] See A. Böhlig and P. Labib, *Die koptisch-gnostische Schrift ohne Titel aus Codex II von Nag Hammadi* (Deutsche Akademie der Wissenschaften zu Berlin, Institut für Orientforschung 58), Berlin 1962, 19ff.

[185] Here again, however, one might draw different conclusions. Irenaeus, distinct from the other versions, seems to have written of 'the first Man and

Although it is not, then, possible to come to a firm conclusion regarding the status of the reference to the Son of Man in this well-known response to the demiurge's blasphemy, it is necessary to point out that, even if the mention of the Son of Man be understood as an addition to the most original tradition, one need not conclude that the addition must be the result of Christian influence. These narratives all speak of an *image* of the heavenly Man according to which the first man of the earth was formed. As is well known, there was much speculation by Philo and others concerning the independent existence of this image. This image might itself be regarded as the first heavenly Man, but, when the high God himself or one of his emanations could be spoken of as first Man who himself had a heavenly image (as is true in these and other gnostic materials), it may well have been felt necessary to offer some designation for this image. Given the frequent coupling of 'man' and 'son of man' in the traditional language of Judaism along with the Semitic understanding that such a mention of the Son of Man was, in one sense, but another way of speaking of the Man[186] seen in a different aspect, one could readily understand how such language might have been adapted in Jewish-gnostic or pre-gnostic cosmogonic and anthropogonic speculations.

Some corroboration for this possibility may be given when this context for reference to the Son of Man is examined. This image of the heavenly Man, who is often called the Son of Man, is not identified with the Christ or his traditional functions. Not only does this gnostic Son of Man not undertake any of the roles

---

Man, Son of Man'. (So the Latin; in the portion of the Greek which has been passed on to us καὶ ἄνθρωπος must be supplied.) If this correctly reflects Irenaeus' language, one might come to believe that Irenaeus knew of two variant statements of the retort to Ialdabaoth, which he then combined, or that he might have been working with a version which had interpolated a reference to the Son of Man. In this latter case, however, it might seem surprising that none of the other versions has preserved indications of the secondary character of this statement.

Alternatively, Irenaeus may have himself attempted, consciously or unconsciously, to interpret what he found before him, perhaps in a Christian fashion by identifying the Son of Man, Jesus, with the Man. Possibly, also, he has preserved a more Semitic understanding in which the Son of Man is understood to be a counterpart or an appositional way of speaking about the Man and not a distinct entity. See also above, p. 73, on a Naassene presentation which could preserve an older realization that Man and Son of Man were two ways of speaking of the same figure.

186 On these issues, see below, pp. 116ff.

ascribed to the Son of Man of the Gospels (eschatological judge, ministry on earth, sufferer), but he also plays no independent role in the creation. Despite Christian references to the only-begotten and the son of the father to be found elsewhere in the Apocryphon, we cannot too readily assume that the Apocryphon's Son of Man was always identified with the Christian Son of God in the gnostic mind.[187]

An intriguing further use of Son of Man language is found in another context in the 'long' version of the Apocryphon. The understanding expressed in all four versions seems to be that Adam, after the introduction of sexual intercourse and other corruptions into the world, awakened to himself and his true origin. He then realized that he must bring forth a true son, who would not be created through sexual intercourse, and who then could be the head of a race of true men. In the Berlin codex version it is said that Adam, recognizing his own οὐσία, brought forth Seth.[188] In the 'short' version we read: 'But when Adam knew the image of his Prognosis, he brought forth the image of the Son of Man (*pshēre mprōme*). He called him Seth.'[189] No Christian influences are here evident, and it is very likely that an allusion to Gen. 5.3 (Adam 'became the father of a son in his own likeness, after his image, and named him Seth') stands behind this view. In this event, it would be Adam who was here seen as the Son of Man. In these circumstances one may well suppose that it is the 'long' version with its use of 'image' (*eine*)[190] which stands closer to the original Semitic thought and that a reference to the Son of Man as Adam could have been dropped by a Christian composer or

[187] Giversen (*Apocryphon Johannis*, 239f.), however, does argue for this identification. He points to CG II, 6.15f., which speaks, he believes, of the Christian anointed one, of the only son of the Metropator (the parallels in the 'short' version do not speak of the 'great father' as such here). He then points to CG II, 5.6f., where the Metropator and first Man are linked. (We do not find that they are here identified and, indeed, this Metropator is not the gnostic, unknown, high God, since he exists below the Mother of All.) While we would, of course, agree that these gnostics saw Christ as the son of a father who might at times be seen in the guise of the Man, this does not, for the reasons given above and below, guarantee that the image of the Man above was understood as the Christ in all gnostic contexts.

[188] BG 8502, 63.12–14. CG III, 32.6–8, gives a different reading which is difficult to interpret, cf. Till's edition of BG 8502, 167.

[189] CG II, 24.35–25.1; IV, 38.24–28.

[190] 'Image', 'likeness', 'form'. The Coptic word is often used in passages which ultimately depend on the *ṣelem* and (especially) *dᵉmūt* language found both in Gen. 1.26 and 5.3. Cf. CG II, 14.24; 15.3, 10; 19.31.

redactor of the 'short' version. Indeed, such an understanding may help us at last to realize the basis for other references to 'the son of the Son of Man' and to 'the seed of the Son of Man'. At one stage in gnostic tradition it may well have been Seth and his descendants[191] (i.e. the true gnostics) who were thus indicated.

It is important also to realize that in the gnostic thought world, a figure like Seth is not to be understood solely as an earthly being. Earlier in the Apocryphon we hear of the procession (from out of the Prognosis, the perfect Nous, through the revelation of the will of the invisible spirit and the Autogenes) of the perfect Man (*rōme τέλειος*). His name is Adamas,[192] and he is placed over the first aeon (together with the great Autogenes, Christ).[193] The son Seth is then established over the second aeon.[194]

Seth's role is understood in a parallel fashion in the Gospel of the Egyptians. Adamas has come forth from the first Man.[195] Later we hear several times of the incorruptible Seth, the son of the incorruptible Man (*pshēre mpaphthartos nrōme*).[196] If it serves no other purpose, these references may help us to understand that some gnostics did not always think in Christian terms when they wrote or spoke of the Son of Man.

3. CONCLUDING REMARKS

It is evident from our survey of the materials that the Son of Man designation was, relatively speaking, much more popular among gnostic Christians and perhaps among non-Christian gnostics than it was among those Christians who were not heavily influenced by

[191] Among the published Nag Hammadi documents the importance of the sons or race of Seth is especially clear in the Apocalypse of Adam (see below, p. 105 n. 203), a work which may be non-Christian in its entirety and which probably reaches back into much earlier Jewish, baptismal sectarian circumstances.

[192] Adamas in CG III, 13.4; Adaman in CG II, 8.35; Adam in BG 8502, 35.5.

[193] Cf. CG II, 8.23–9.2; CG III, 12.24–13.7; BG 8502, 34.19–35.8. This and the following are lacking in a badly preserved section of CG IV.

The passage in parentheses might well be suspect as a Christian interpolation into these gnostic views.

[194] CG II, 9.11; CG III, 13.17f.; BG 8502, 35.21.

[195] CG III, 49.8–10. In connection with some of our earlier comparative materials, it is significant to recognize with Doresse that important sections of this Gospel are concerned with baptism, the last part 'recalls undoubtedly a baptismal liturgy'. *Secret Books*, 179.

[196] CG III, 51.20f. = CG IV, 63.15–17; CG III, 55.16–18.

gnostic understandings. Even though we continue to face a plethora of unsolved questions about influences, backgrounds and relationships, this much is clear no matter how the evidence is otherwise analysed and no matter what other reservations one may wish to introduce. The witness of Irenaeus and Hippolytus to the gnostic use of the designation is supported by a significant number of the extant gnostic writings. Over twenty sectarian groups and/or authors have brought themselves to our attention in this connection.

It would also appear that, for the most part, the usage of the Son of Man title among the gnostics was not directly dependent upon the Son of Man sayings now contained in the canonical Gospels, however much this gnostic usage may otherwise depend on Christian tradition. In the materials here studied only Gospel of Thomas, logion 86; fragment from Heracleon 35; *Excerpta ex Theodoto* 4.3; 61.4 and two statements drawn by Hippolytus from the Peratae (*Refutation* V.12.7; 16.11) are extant as Son of Man sayings which indicate some form of relationship with Son of Man logia now found in the canonical Gospels. 'On the Resurrection' (CG I) 46.15f. might also be understood to show such a relationship, though in a more tangential fashion.[197] In addition, the Clementine *Recognitions* I.60.3 and *Homilies* III.22.3 along with the quotation from Monoïmus in Hippolytus, *Refutation* VIII.13.2, and Gospel of Mary (BG 8502) 8.18 reveal the influence of materials now found in the New Testament, though otherwise not directly associated with the Son of Man. The statement with regard to Marcosian beliefs in Irenaeus' *Against Heresies* I.15.3 and the sayings in Gospel of Mary (BG 8502) 9.9 and the Sophia of Jesus Christ (BG 8502) 101.7 par. (similarly in the Epistle of Eugnostos, CG III, 81.12–14) refer to established New Testament incidents or themes (baptism of Jesus, kingdom), but without otherwise employing phraseology known from canonical writings. The remainder of the gnostic-type Son of Man materials which we have studied indicate none of these direct or indirect influences with any clarity. They might, however, be subdivided into three further categories, though not without reservations in particular instances:

[197] To this list some might wish to append Gospel of Philip, saying 54, which begins 'Even so came the Son of Man . . .' in a fashion common to several canonical Son of Man sayings, though in other respects the themes and language are quite different. Cf. above p. 6 n. 22; p. 26 n. 89.

(1) statements in which the language bears a Christian imprint, due either to their formation by Christian gnostics or to their Christianization;[198] (2) statements which themselves reveal no definite Christian themes, but which are found in (or were drawn from) materials either of Christian-gnostic origin or which appear to have been Christianized;[199] (3) at least two of the sayings from the Epistle of Eugnostos (CG III, 81.21f. par.; 85.9f. par.) which display no Christian ideas and which might be regarded as portions of a wholly non-Christian treatise.

Whatever attempts we make at classification, however, it is evident, by any standard, that we are dealing with heterogeneous traditions for which assured common denominators are hard to come by. Nevertheless, there are questions for which we may attempt, at this stage in the study of the Nag Hammadi documents, provisional answers. One of the chief among them might be posed in these terms: Why does the Son of Man expression occur so much more frequently in gnostic-Christian writings than in those of a more orthodox nature? Is it (*a*) due to a tradition of use created by the canonical evangelists and/or the traditions which stand immediately behind the canonical Gospels? Or (*b*) is it due to a yet earlier Christian usage which then developed in different forms in gnostic Christianity from those which were finally preserved in the canonical Gospels? Or (*c*) is it due in some measure to a non-Christian usage, i.e. either an essentially Jewish-gnostic tradition

[198] Clem. *Rec.* III.61.2; Hippolytus, *Refut.* V.7.33; 26.30; Gospel of Philip, sayings 54; 102; 120; On the Resurrection (CG I) 44.23, 30f.; *Sophia Jesu Christi* (BG 8502) 98.11f. par.; 124.2, 6 par. There are two further references from works as yet unpublished at this writing which should be included in this category. In what has been called the Paraphrase of Shem, but which is in reality two treatises, the second one being the Second Tractate of the Great Seth (CG VII/2, 49.10–70.12; cf. Robinson, *NTS* 14, 1967/8, 379) where the passage of interest is found, we read: 'These things, it is I who told them to you, I, Jesus Christ, son of the Man who is higher than the heavens, O ye perfect and stainless . . .' See Doresse, *Secret Books*, 149, and Schenke, *Gott* 'Mensch', 15, who notes that, on the basis of Doresse's translation, 'who is higher than the heavens' could refer either to the Man or the son. The whole statement might be read as a late and rather self-conscious attempt to link Jesus with the Man's son. The second passage is found in CG IX/3, a tractate without title, as now presented a Christian work: 'What is revealed to us by the Son of Man is that we must receive the word of truth.' See Doresse, *op. cit.*, 220.

[199] Irenaeus, *Adv. Haer.* I.12.4 (twice); I.30.1, 6; Hippolytus, *Refut.* V.6.4; VIII.12.2; 13.3, 4 (4 times); Apoc. John (CG II) 44.15 parr.; 25.1 par.; *Sophia Jesu Christi* (BG 8502) 102.15 par.; 108.2 par.; Gospel of the Egyptians (CG III) 59.2–4.

which never directly affected first-century Christianity or a pre-Christian tradition which in part affected early Christianity and in part was carried on into gnostic lore?

As we read the evidence, it may well be necessary to reckon with all of these causes, since the imprint of (*a*) above does not seem sufficient to account for all the materials we have studied. Of course, it can be argued that Gnosticism has made drastic revisions in the material from the canonical Gospels which refers to the Son of Man – that their different concerns and interests have caused them radically to recast canonical traditions. If this be true, however, the revision has been carried through so thoroughly in a significant number of instances as almost to obliterate all traces of connection in terms of theme, intent and the form and vocabulary of the sayings. (Not only is this true in terms of a relationship with synoptic logia about the Son of Man, but it is also true with regard to the Johannine sayings with which the gnostics, at least at first glance, might appear to have had more in common.) It would appear that, as also with the more orthodox Christian materials discussed earlier in our study, there was passed on to gnostic Christianity neither the proper context for nor the incentive to worship or proclaim Jesus as the Son of Man in terms of conceptions now found in the canonical Gospels.

The causes for this demise are probably easier to understand with respect to the gnostics than to the more orthodox writers.[200] Eschatological statements about the Son of Man would have been of little value to groups who saw no meaning in the historical process and who looked for salvation, not in the future, but in another realm. Similarly, statements about the Son of Man as a historical earthly figure would have been relatively meaningless to those who saw the saviour primarily as a heavenly revealer whose visit to earth was only for the purposes of disclosing eternal secrets and not to forgive sins (as Mark 2.10 parr.), eat and drink (as Matt. 11.19 par.) and have no place to lay his head (as Matt. 8.20 par.).[201] Finally, the idea that the saviour should actually suffer would have been tantamount to blasphemy to many gnostics.[202]

[200] Cf. above, pp. 56f.
[201] The exception, of course, remains the parallel to Matt. 8.20 in Gospel of Thomas, log. 86, where, however, the logion is given a gnostic wrinkle which probably accounts for its use.
[202] In works which stand somewhat closer to orthodox Christianity,

It is conceivable, however, that, while gnostics made little use of canonical Son of Man logia, they nevertheless did borrow the designation itself from canonical sources. While such an hypothesis could, no doubt, account for some of our evidence, it still does not appeal to us as adequate. Not only does there remain the problem of the absence of other indications (in terms of form and vocabulary) of the contexts from which the title would have been excerpted, but, in a significant number of instances, there is no effort to indicate that the cosmic Son of Man who is mentioned (and rarely elaborated upon) is to be understood as the heavenly Jesus. Even when this is done (as in the central sections of the *Sophia Jesu Christi* and in Irenaeus' *Against Heresies* I.12.4), it is often accomplished in a manner which might well indicate a later and not wholly satisfactory attempt to make an identification.

Furthermore, as we have come to realize in the previous chapter of this study, there are few signs that more orthodox Christian thinkers of the early second century were continuing to employ Son of Man language. This would cause us to question any hypothesis which suggests a borrowing of the title by gnostics from contemporary Christians who themselves were preserving and developing earlier Son of Man references.

We would, therefore, suggest that a significant number of the gnostic references to the Son of Man ought not to be regarded as stemming from the influence of canonical materials. Indeed, such may stand as the most important and provocative result of our discussions.

We are led on, then, to the second of the possibilities – that gnostic usage of the Son of Man designation, in part, derives from forms of early Christian tradition which then developed differently from those which eventually reached the canonical evangelists. We have already pointed to several sayings which might best find their origin in Christian materials which had not yet been codified into Gospels and such might but suggest the outlines of the true dimensions of the issue. This, of course, is a fascinating consideration, though it would be difficult to delineate in detail for the very reason that gnostic-Christian and canonical Christian Son of Man

---

however, such as the Gospels of Truth and of Philip, room is made for some stress upon the cross, though there is still no sign of any Son of Man passion logia.

logia have been developed along such different lines in rather dissimilar contexts.

In this connection we would, however, point out two sets of significant characteristics regarding many of the gnostic references to the Son of Man. We have noticed that a number of the pericopes, from all the categories set out above, have disclosed explicit or implicit associations with liturgical motifs (especially those having to do with baptismal themes) and/or that the writings in which they are found betray a connection with groups which appear, at least at one time, to have practised baptismal customs.[203] It is also important to realize, in this regard, that a number of these groups appear to have their roots in forms of Jewish or semi-Jewish sectarianism in the Palestinian area.[204] We also find it significant that all the gnostic Son of Man sayings placed in categories (2) and (3) above (i.e. statements which reveal no normative Christian themes, whether or not they are located in the context of Christian or Christianized gnostic writings) are cosmogonic and/or anthropogonic in character. This is also true of several of the statements which are clearly Christian or Christianized.

It is within a context concerned both with baptismally oriented themes and customs and with a form of anthropogonic (to a lesser extent cosmogonic) interests that we have elsewhere suggested one might look for the earliest setting of a number of the Son of Man logia now found in the canonical Gospels.[205] Should one wish

---

[203] On further evidence for a native Syrian-Palestinian baptismal sectarianism, under both Jewish and Iranian influence, as a precursor for themes woven deeply into the Apocalypse of Adam (CG V/5), see A. Böhlig, 'Jüdisches und Iranisches in der Adamapokalypse des Codex V von Nag Hammadi', in his *Mysterion und Wahrheit*, 149ff., and his introduction to the Apocalypse in *Koptisch-gnostische Apokalypsen aus Codex V von Nag Hammadi im koptischen Museum zu Alt-Kairo* (A. Böhlig and P. Labib: Wissenschaftliche Zeitschrift der Martin-Luther-Universität, Sonderband), Halle-Wittenberg 1963, 86–95.

[204] After noting Schenke's view that certain Jewish elements in Christian gnostic systems could have entered Gnosticism through Christian influence, R. McL. Wilson yet maintains that 'where the Christian elements are often a mere veneer, the Jewish are generally integrated into the system' (*Gnosis and the New Testament*, Philadelphia 1968, 142). 'These and other facts suggest that the earliest beginnings of the movement are to be sought in Jewish circles, probably in Palestine or Syria rather than Alexandria . . .' (*op. cit.*, 144). On this theme and the transformation of Jewish materials in Gnosticism, cf. further Böhlig, 'Der jüdische und judenchristliche Hintergrund . . .', in *Le Origini dello Gnosticismo*, 109ff.

[205] See *SMMH*, especially ch. V, VII and VIII.

to consider this possibility that certain strands of gnostic tradition could tell us about forms of belief maintained by some early Christians, one might then also ask if the traditions preserved by the canonical Gospels have not tended to develop more explicit historical aspects and to enrich the eschatological characteristics of statements which once had a more decided mythological and liturgical frame of reference.[206]

This, however, leads us on to the third possibility which could also be regarded as a corollary to the alternative outline above. We would here ask whether Gnosticism may have lent its own interpretation to strands of tradition involving the Son of Man designation which once had roots in the language of Jewish sectarianism. Though certain of these Jewish ideas may have affected Christian origins, other aspects of their thought might have passed through channels quite independent of Christianity.

We would first point to the likelihood that Judaism knew of a heavenly Son of Man who was viewed as primarily an eschatological judge and champion.[207] He was, of course, associated in heaven with God himself, the Ancient of Days, whose 'raiment was white as snow, and the hair of his head like pure wool'.[208] This phraseology could indicate that God, too, as elsewhere in the Old Testament, might be conceived of as a kind of super human-like being.[209] It would also appear that this eschatological champion could alternatively be spoken of as one who 'had the appearance of a man'[210] or who 'possessed' 'something like the figure of a man'[211] after which he might be spoken of as 'that Son of

---

[206] Additional words of R. McL. Wilson are worth quoting here: 'Christianity emerged on the stage of history in much the same period (as the earlier forms leading to Gnosticism). It is therefore reasonable to assume that the factors which promoted the development of Gnosticism also had some influence on the emergent Christian faith. Such influence, however, need not have operated in the same way, or produced the same results' (*op. cit.*, 144).

[207] The view that it was the church which first gave titular status to the designation is now most forcibly argued by Perrin, *Rediscovering the Teaching of Jesus*, 164ff. He would evidently regard the references to the Son of Man in I Enoch and to the Man in II Esdras as forms of parallel development. As one argument against this possibility, cf. again Borsch, *NTS* 14, 1967/8, 565ff.

[208] Dan. 7.9. See I Enoch 46.1.

[209] Cf. Ezek. 1.26, on which see *SMMH*, 137f.

[210] I Enoch 46.1.

[211] II Esd. 13.3.

Man' or 'that Man'. In our earlier study we have proposed that these conceptions and the lore with which they are found in context may have depended, in association with Dan. 7.13f., on far older mythological and cultic understandings concerning the royal Man who ascends to assume rule on a throne imagined to be in heaven. However this thesis is assessed, it is at least conceivable that Gnosticism, in its conception of a divine Man under whom there existed a divine Son of Man, was in part influenced by forms of Jewish eschatological picture language. The eschatological context for the figures would then have been lost, as may well also have been the case for many other themes and motifs borrowed by Gnosticism from earlier Jewish beliefs and hopes.[212]

There is, however, another (perhaps related) form of explanation which might better suit the contexts in which a number of the gnostic references to the Man and the Son of Man are found. The cosmogonic and anthropogonic interests of the gnostics frequently have an obvious basis in speculation centred upon the first several chapters of Genesis. The crucial verses for this speculation were, of course, Gen. 1.26f., which begin: 'Then God said, "Let us make man in our image, after our likeness; and let them have dominion . . ." '

Jewish thinkers and writers commented frequently on the nature of this image and upon the implications of 'them'. There was also an apologetic concern with the implications of the 'us' and 'our'. Jervell is doubtless right when he argues that most Jews were loath to entertain any form of speculation which might challenge the absolute supremacy and uniqueness of God. Thus, while there was certainly an interest in the intermediary figure of Wisdom, there is little or no direct evidence that Palestinian Jews thought in terms of an independent man-like heavenly image or a heavenly man made after that image, though there are indications that the rabbis were aware of gnostic speculations in this regard.[213]

It would certainly appear, however, that a number of the gnostics,[214] a Pauline disciple and/or Paul himself,[215] along with

---

[212] On the use of language and imagery from Jewish eschatology by the gnostics, see R. M. Grant, *Gnosticism and Early Christianity*, New York 1959.

[213] J. Jervell, *Imago Dei: Gen. 1.26f. im Spätjudentum, in der Gnosis und in den paulinischen Briefen* (FRLANT, nF 58), 1960, 15ff.; 71ff.

[214] See also Schenke, *Gott 'Mensch'*, especially 69ff.; 120ff.

[215] See II Cor. 4.4; Col. 1.15ff.; compare Heb. 1.3.

the author of the Poimandres[216] and Philo[217] thought in terms of a heavenly Man-image or a heavenly Man made in this image, and that in so doing they were largely or in part influenced by these verses from Genesis. The existence of such traditions might either point to some earlier form of belief or to the influence of Hellenistic and to some extent Christian transformational influences.

Another form of this thought seems to be present in Jewish-Hellenistic writings which exalted Adam to a heavenly position. While more orthodox Jewish writers were largely content to glorify Adam as an earthly creature,[218] such writings as the Life of Adam and Eve,[219] the Apocalypse of Moses[220] and the Testament of Abraham[221] also knew of him as a heavenly being.

These several forms of tradition may be regarded as having had an influence upon Gnosticism or having shared with Gnosticism common sources of influence. There was, in many of these speculations, a heavenly Man who had an image according to which the first earthly man was made. In some instances, as we have seen, the speculation apparently led to the belief that the heavenly Man could be identified with God; in other cases the Man was one of the emanations of the highest deity. In either event, the Man was himself held to have this image, a counterpart, or, if you will, a kind of son, who often seems to have required some form of identity.

In one mythical version it would appear that the Man was known as the heavenly Adam or Adamas. Also his son, the son of Adam, Seth (who is once said to have been made in the image of the Son of Man), could be regarded as a heavenly hero.[222] It is perhaps as the result of similar thought that in the Jewish-Hellenistic Testament of Abraham, not only Adam is pictured sitting on the throne of judgment ('and the appearance of the Man [ἄνθρωπος] was terrible, like unto that of the Lord . . . this all-

---

[216] *Corpus Hermeticum* I.12.

[217] See Jervell, *op. cit.*, 52ff.; *SMMH*, 170ff. E.g. *Leg. alleg.* I.53, 88; *De conf. ling.* 41, 146, 147.

[218] But one who is a 'second angel' (II Enoch 30.10) and who, when created, extended from one end of the world to the other, his stature reaching to the heavens, and who filled the whole earth (Gen. Rabba 8.1; 21.3). See further *SMMH*, 108f.; Schenke, *Gott* 'Mensch', 125ff., especially with reference to the rabbinic use of Gen. 1.26f.

[219] Ch. 33.

[220] Ch. 39.

[221] See below.

[222] See above, pp. 109f.

marvellous Man' [ἀνήρ]),²²³ but also his son Abel, the son of Adam (υἱὸς 'Aδάμ), sits on a fiery, crystal throne, 'a wondrous Man (ἀνήρ), shining as the sun, like unto a son of God'.²²⁴ In our earlier study we have suggested that at a distance behind these several presentations there stands the ancient conception of the royal person who comes to the throne as a representative of his ancestor, the first king of the world. In one sense, the son is, of course, a distinct personage, but, in another view, he is his father manifested again in a new form. Seen in one frame of reference, this royal succession takes place upon the earth, but the process was also sometimes viewed as having a counterpart in the heavenly realm. We would propose that this ancient understanding may have been working itself out in different ways in the forms which we have before us.

That the one descendant from the Man should be called the Son of Man could also be explained by the fact that the two terms *man* and *son of man* are frequently linked in other contexts in Judaism. There the reference is normally, of course, to the man's creatureliness and dependence; in a number of instances explicit comparison is made with God's greatness and immortality.²²⁵ Since, however, the gnostics were capable of thinking of *man* as a heavenly being, there would be no reason why the *son of man* could not similarly be exalted. As we have noted, this had already happened in Jewish eschatological thought, and the reference in II Esdras 13.3 to the Man who comes out of the heart of the sea and flies with the clouds of heaven reminds us again of just how interchangeable the expressions had been in the Semitic thought world.²²⁶

What is more, there are at least two Old Testament passages which see the man/son of man in a far more significant role. There

²²³ Long rec. XI; see short rec. VIII.
²²⁴ Long rec. VIII.
²²⁵ See Num. 23.19; Job 16.21; 25.6; 35.8; Ps. 144.3; Isa. 51.12; 56.2; Jer. 49.18, 33; 50.40; 51.43; Ecclus. 17.30 (men/son of man); Judith 8.16; Test. Joseph 2.5. The Hebrew expressions are alternatively *'enōš, ben 'ādām* (once *'ādām, ben 'enōš*, once *geber, ben 'ādām*) and *'iš, ben 'ādām*.
²²⁶ See above, pp. 116f. A number of scholars have also suggested that Paul has several times used the designation *Man* to avoid the Son of Man, which might easily have been misunderstood by Greek-speaking Christians. Cf. *SMMH*, 240ff. We are suggesting, however, that Greek-speaking gnostics, consciously or unconsciously, made use of this Semitic idea in order to create a further emanation.

is Ps. 80.17 with its statement about 'the man of thy right hand, the son of man whom thou hast made strong for thyself', and, of yet more importance for us, Psalm 8. There the language is, of course, strongly reminiscent of Gen. 1.26, which reads: 'Then God said, "Let us make man in our image, after our likeness; and let them have dominion over the fish of the sea, and over the birds of the air, and over the cattle, and over all the earth, and over every creeping thing that creeps upon the earth." ' The relevant verses from Psalm 8 are an expansion and a virtual commentary.

> What is man that thou art mindful of him,
> and the son of man that thou dost care for him?
> Yet thou hast made him little less than *elohim*,
> and dost crown him with glory and honour.
> Thou hast given him dominion over the works of thy hands;
> thou hast put all things under his feet,
>   all sheep and oxen
> and also the beasts of the field,
>   the birds of the air, and the fish of the sea,
> whatever passes along the paths of the sea.
>
> (Ps. 8.4–8)

Later rabbinic speculators were certainly well acquainted with the close relationship between Gen. 1.26f. and Psalm 8.[227] Clearly, since the gnostics were able to think of God or his principal emanation as a heavenly Man with reference to Gen. 1.26f., it would have been possible for them as well to think of the plurals there in the light of the Man and the Son of Man of Ps. 8.4f., who *are* made little less than *God*,[228] crowned with glory and honour.[229] In this connection we would also remind ourselves that in every instance in the gnostic literature where the two expressions are actually joined ('the Man and the Son of Man')[230] or very closely

[227] E.g. Gen. Rabba 8.6.

[228] Or *gods*. Though many later Jews would interpret this as 'angels', the Hebrew word remained for others to interpret as they would.

[229] Pannenberg (*Jesus – God and Man*, 196 n. 1) would also ask, 'Is not the concept of Adam as a being like an angel with a *doxa*-body . . . understandable as an exegesis of Ps. 8.5 ?' See his long and interesting note on this and related questions.

[230] Irenaeus, *Adv. Haer.* I.30.6; Hippolytus, *Refut.* V.6.4; Gospel of Philip, saying 102; Apoc. John (CG II) 14.15 parr.; Gospel of the Egyptians (CG III) 59.2–4; *Sophia Jesu Christi* (BG 8502) 98.11f. par.

associated [231] we are dealing with a distinctly cosmogonic and/or anthropogonic context.

Whether or not Psalm 8 is accorded as much significance as we have given it here, the ready coinage of the Jewish parallel expressions *man* and *son of man* must be recognized. This, together with the honour accorded to the great Adam's Son by his *sons*, the gnostics (and perhaps their precursors), may better explain the place of the Son of Man in a number of gnostic passages where it is Jewish and not Christian thought which appears fundamental. Though numerous questions and gaps in our knowledge remain, it is this hypothesis which will perhaps repay our further study.

[231] Irenaeus, *Adv. Haer.* I.12.4; 15.3; 30.1, 6; Hippolytus, *Refut.* VIII. 12.2; 13.3, 4; Letter of Eugnostos (CG III) 85.9–11.

INDEX OF MODERN AUTHORS

Bold type indicates a first reference to a work by this author

INDEX OF REFERENCES

1. Old Testament

2. Jewish Apocrypha, Pseudepigrapha, Rabbinical and Related Writings

3. *New Testament*

5. Gnostic Literature